TRUTHS THAT TRANSFORM

BY D. James Kennedy

Evangelism Explosion
The God of Great Surprises
This Is the Life
Spiritual Renewal
Truths That Transform

D. James Kennedy

TRUTHS THAT TRANSFORM

Fleming H. Revell Company
Old Tappan, New Jersey

Library of Congress Cataloging in Publication Data

Kennedy, Dennis James, 1930–
    Truths that transform.

    1. Theology, Doctrinal—Popular works.   I.   Title.
BT77.K277   230   74-20923
ISBN 0-8007-0655-2

To my daughter Jennifer
who has been a source of continual joy

CONTENTS

FOREWORD

D. James Kennedy's EVANGELISM EXPLOSION was a book on spreading the gospel, the central concern of every Christian. It became a best seller because in it he showed how every Christian can be an effective witness. The present book, TRUTHS THAT TRANSFORM, is for those who have yearned for a deeper understanding of Christian truth and what it can mean in their lives. It is designed to open your eyes to the spiritual potential in everyday life through a deeper knowledge of the teaching of the Scriptures.

No book can exhaust the truths contained in the Scriptures, but here is a vital guide to finding the central facts which the Bible teaches. More than that, Dr. Kennedy shows how facts can become a living set of truths that will transform your life.

THE PUBLISHERS

PREFACE

In this age of "soda-fizz" theology, it seems to me that there is a great need for more substantial biblical and theological foundations—lest the bubbles burst. In a culture which has become almost entirely experientially oriented, there is a crucial need for the eternal verities of God's Word. I have, therefore, endeavored to set forth in these pages in popular fashion some of the great truths of the historic Christian faith.

These are *Truths That Transform!* The Coral Ridge Presbyterian Church of Fort Lauderdale, Florida, where it has been my joy and privilege for the past fifteen years to minister for Christ, has been for many the proving ground of these truths. They do indeed transform! This church has been noted for the evangelistic ministry of its laymen. Many have asked, "How are such laymen produced?" I am certain that good spiritual nutrition is a vital factor. The great old truths of the faith put iron in men's backbones and enable them to stand tall for Christ. Herein are contained some of the great teachings of Christianity which God has used throughout centuries to bless lives, transform men, and build His Church.

Over the many months during which these chapters were prepared, a vast number of sources were consulted including Augustine, Martin Luther, John Calvin, John Knox, Charles Hodge, A. A. Hodge, Robert Dabney, Charles Shedd, Robert Webb, John Murray, Lorraine Boettner, John Gerstner, Abraham Kuiper, Alexander

Keith, Carl F. H. Henry, Francis Schaeffer and many others too numerous to be mentioned. I am greatly indebted to all of these men for the light which they have shined upon God's Word. Ultimately, we have endeavored to be faithful to the Holy Scriptures, which are the only infallible rule of faith and practice and which are to be the final authority in all matters of religion.

I would like to express my deep appreciation to Cay Hunter, Virginia Shaw, and my excellent secretary Ruth Rohm, for their fine work in editing the manuscript. Of course, whatever errors or mistakes there may be are fully my responsibility.

I send this manuscript off with the heartfelt prayer that God may be pleased to use it for the upbuilding and strengthening of His Kingdom and the glory of His Name.

Soli Deo Gloria!

D. JAMES KENNEDY

TRUTHS THAT TRANSFORM

1 THE SOVEREIGNTY OF GOD

Remember the former things of old: for I am God, and there is none else; I am God, and there is none like me, Declaring the end from the beginning, and from ancient times the things that are not yet done, saying, My counsel shall stand, and I will do all my pleasure: Calling a ravenous bird from the east, the man that executeth my counsel from a far country: yea, I have spoken it, I will also bring it to pass; I have purposed it, I will also do it.

Isaiah 46:9–11

"Your God is altogether too human," wrote Luther to the famous Renaissance humanist scholar Erasmus. I feel certain the great Dutch scholar was greatly offended at such an accusation, but history and a casual investigation of Scripture reveal the accusation to be true. In our day, J. B. Phillips has hurled the same accusation at mankind in the title of his book, *Your God Is Too Small*. With this thought in mind, I want to ask the question: Who rules the world in which you live—the world you read about on the front page of our newspaper? How big is your God?

I realize that the sovereignty of God is not a popular subject. It never has been and never will be. Since the beginning of creation, the creature has sought to usurp the place of the Creator. This was seen in Lucifer, the angel of light, who tried to become like God and take upon himself the prerogatives of God. For this reason, he was cast out of heaven and a great multitude of angels with him. It was this same sin that brought the whole human race into its present disgraceful and depraved condition. Man wanted to usurp the authority of God and be the god of his own life. He was unwilling to listen to the words of Him who said, "Thus far shalt thou go and no further . . . thou shalt not eat. . . ." But the creature reached out a rebellious hand, took, ate, and died!

Genesis 2:17

The skeptic H. G. Wells said that the world is like a great stage production produced and managed by God. As the curtain goes up, all is lovely to behold. The characters are fantastically beautiful—a delight to both eye and ear. All goes well until the leading man steps on the hem of the leading lady's dress. She then trips over a chair and knocks over a lamp which pushes over a table into the side wall. This knocks over the back scenery, which brings the whole thing crashing down in chaos on the heads of the actors! Meanwhile behind the scenes, God, the Producer, is frantically running to and fro, pulling strings and shouting orders, trying desperately to restore order to the chaos but—ah!—alas! He's unable to do so! Poor God! This is the God of modern man, a very little, limited God. "Either God is not good or He is not powerful," said one unbeliever, "otherwise the world could not be in the mess it's in." Since most people are unwilling to believe God is not good, they conclude He is not all powerful. He's doing the best He can, but His best isn't good enough! He is the God who tries and fails. Which horn of this dilemma do you choose?

May I suggest an alternative? The reason for the mess the world is in is not because God is not good, or not able. The problem is man. He is not good or able. Consider for a moment a trip to hell. After arriving and surveying the awful scene, you would see nothing but misery and woe. You might conclude God is not good or able, otherwise He would not allow such a place of misery. But your conclusion would be wrong. It is precisely because God is good, holy, just, and because He is all powerful, that these wicked, sinful, and rebellious men had been cast into hell.

Many people worship a limited God, but close scrutiny reveals He is not the God of Scripture. The God of the Bible is the omnipotent Creator and Ruler of the world!

If the Old Testament presents anything of God, it presents three attributes: First, the *omnipotence of God,* He has all power and therefore His plan will be worked out. Second, the *holiness of God,* He is holy and therefore His plan, which will be and is being worked out, is one which is morally right. Third, the *personality of God,* He is not some mere omnipotent force as the fatalist would maintain, but He is a Person who is infinite, whose attributes are love, mercy, wisdom, righteousness, justice, goodness, and truth. God is a Person who is all powerful and all holy.

The biblical picture is not one of fatalism because fatalism puts the world's fate into the hands of an impersonal force. The Bible puts the world's fate into the hands of God, the Father, who is all righteous, all wise, and all merciful. Fatalism rules out all second causes, whereas the Bible establishes them. Philosophers have never been able to reconcile human freedom with divine sovereignty. The Bible declares man, in a certain sense, is free. He is free to do whatever he *pleases,* though he is not free in his natural state to do what he *ought* because he is bound by sin and thus is the bondslave of sin. But he is free to do whatever he wants which is man's great problem when his heart and mind are depraved.

Many people see the world as a driverless chariot, horses running wild, reins flapping in the wind, about to plummet off the edge of the road into the abyss. The Scripture presents a God who has the reins of this world firmly in His hands, who is in absolute control of all things, who is working out His perfect plan for the world. The Scripture says: ". . . My counsel shall stand, and I will do all my pleasure . . . yea, I have spoken it, I will also bring it to pass; I have purposed it, and I will also do it." Sinful man flaunts the so-called autocracy of his own human will. He supposes himself to have veto power over the plans of the Almighty.

Isaiah 46:9–11

Some believe that God submits and man permits; that God can do only that which man allows Him. How ludicrous to think that Almighty God, who by His very Word caused the galaxies of the universe to leap into being, should be governed by His creation—like some mighty mouse who lifts his finger to the Almighty Infinite God and says, "Thus far and no further shalt Thou go." Blasphemy! And unfortunately many Christians cry with the humanists: "I am the master of my fate and the captain of my soul."

Proverbs 21:1

Mark 14:30

Proverbs 16:33

1 Samuel 14:42

Book of Jonah

Acts 1:24, 26

Job 36:32 RSV

1 Kings 22:28, 34

Job 14:5

This is not the biblical picture. According to Scripture, God controls everything from the mightiest galaxy to the most infinitesimal atom. He controls the angels in heaven, the inhabitants of earth, and the kings and fortunes of nations. He raises them up and casts them down. He brings one to power and then removes it by a stroke of His hand. The Bible says: "The king's heart is in the hand of the Lord, as the rivers of water: he turneth it whithersoever he will." God sets up nations and sets the basest of men to rule over them. God controls planets and nations as well as the dumb beasts of earth. He said that before the cock would crow twice, Peter would deny Him thrice—and it happened!

We see that God even controls what men call fortuitous events, because in God's economy there is nothing called luck, chance, or fate. The living God controls all things. Proverbs 16:33 says: "The lot is cast into the lap; but the whole disposing thereof is of the Lord." In 1 Samuel 14:42 when they cast lots, the lot fell on Jonathan because God controlled the casting of the lot. In the Book of Jonah, the lot fell on Jonah. In Acts 1:24, 26 after the disciples prayed, they said: "Thou Lord, which knowest the hearts of all men, shew whether of these two thou hast chosen . . . . And they gave forth their lots; and the lot fell upon Matthias . . . ." People suppose that lightning is certainly an uncontrolled happenstance, a freak of nature, an accident. But the Bible says, "[God] covers his hands with the lightning, and commands it to strike the mark."

How about an event as fortuitous as shooting an arrow at random? The prophet said: "If thou [Ahab] return at all in peace, the Lord hath not spoken by me." And then a soldier took up his bow and shot an arrow into the air and smote the king of Israel between the joints of his armor. God is in control of all things in this world. The tiniest events of our lives are in His hands. Even our days are numbered. As Job 14:5 says: "Seeing his days are determined, the number of his months are with thee, thou hast appointed his bounds that he cannot pass."

The Bible clearly points out that God controls the spirits of all men which He hath created. As I have stated, the king's heart is in the hand of Jehovah as the rivers of water. He turneth it whithersoever He will. A man's goings are established by Jehovah.

God demonstrated His tremendous power in Egypt when He sent an angel to destroy the firstborn in every house of the Egyptians. And lest the Egyptians rise up and slay all the Jews, God showed His power by saying: "But against any of the children of Israel shall not a dog move his tongue, against man or beast: that ye may know how that the Lord doth put a difference between the Egyptians and Israel."

Exodus 11:7

God controls the free acts of men. "For it is God which worketh in you both to will and to do of his good pleasure." Jehovah gave the people favor in the sight of the Egyptians so that they let them leave to worship their God. God further showed He was in control when He caused the Egyptians not to retaliate against the Jews but so worked in their hearts that they lent the Israelites their gold and silver and precious stones.

Philippians 2:13

Exodus 12:35, 36

God's sovereignty was again displayed when the Israelites lived in the land of Canaan among a hostile people whose land they had taken and who wanted to take it back again. But God, showing His mighty control over the hearts of men, arranged it so that the Canaanites would not even so much as desire the land while the men were gone to worship in Jerusalem. So, three times a year, year after year, century after century, every able-bodied man in Palestine left his home open to the Hittite, Canaanite, and the Amorite and went to Jerusalem. God so controlled their hearts that they could not so much as even desire the land.

Some people believe God can't convert a soul unless that soul gives Him permission. I wish they would ask the Apostle Paul, that great hater and despiser of Christ and His Church, who, while on his way to Damascus to persecute the Christians, was suddenly cast to the ground by God and converted. The Bible also says that God opened the heart of Lydia and caused her to attend unto the things that were spoken by Paul. "Thy people shall be willing in the day of thy power . . . ."

Acts 16:14
Psalms 110:3

It is only God who can change the human heart. He has determined to save His elect and He will do exactly that. "All that the Father giveth me shall come to me . . . . No man can come to me, except the Father which hath sent me draw him." But after the example of Lucifer and Adam, sinful man still throws his autocratic will into the face of God. But hear the reply of the Almighty: "So then it is not of him that willeth, nor of him that runneth, but of God that

John 6:37, 44

Romans 9:16, 18

sheweth mercy . . . . Therefore hath he mercy on whom he will have mercy, and whom he will he hardeneth." Over against the constant and repeated invitation to come to Christ, there needs to be set forth the balance of the divine sovereignty. Though the outward commandments of Christ may be flaunted, ignored, despised, and disobeyed, the secret counsel of Jehovah is coming to pass and He will make the very wrath of men to praise Him.

There is no man nor group of men who could oppose, frustrate, or limit any purpose of God. The Scripture says that when all the Gentiles, together with the Jews and their rulers, shall set themselves to oppose God and His Christ, God, "that sitteth in the heavens shall laugh: the Lord shall

Psalms 2:4

have them in derision." God is God and not man and He doeth whatsoever He pleases in this earth, and there is none that can speak against Him!

Is there unrighteousness then with God? God forbid. For what does God do? He looks down upon mankind and sees everyone of us has sinned and transgressed His law. ". . . There is none righteous, no, not one . . . . They

Romans 3:10, 12

are together become unprofitable . . . ." "The heart is deceitful above all things, and desperately wicked: who can

Jeremiah 17:9, 10

know it? I the Lord search the heart . . . ." Therefore, God would be absolutely just if He brought a flood and once again inundated the earth. God would not be unrighteous; He would merely be a Judge passing a just sentence upon wicked men. But God in His great mercy condescended to extend grace to a vast multitude whom no man can number and sent His Son to redeem those whom the Father hath given Him. Furthermore, God's purposes for each always will be done.

This is seen in the story of Joseph. His foolish and prejudiced father acted according to his own nature and gave him a coat of many colors and other preferential tokens. The foolish boy boasted to his brothers, and the brothers, according to their own evil natures, were jealous and sold him into slavery. The slave traders, according to their own greed and evil nature, bought him. Potiphar, out of a desire for gain in his household, took and made him a servant in his house. Potiphar's wife, out of lust and lasciviousness, sought to seduce him and, when he refused, had him cast into prison. But Joseph was raised up to be prime minister of Egypt and when his brethren came for food, he said: "Ye

Genesis 50:20

did it for evil; but God meant it for good."

God overrules and permits the evil acts of men so His grace will infallibly be extended to those for whom it is ordained. His justice will inevitably come upon those who reject His Son; those who are fitted for destruction. And God's glory will be manifested. Charles Spurgeon said that they would have a God who enters into His workroom and creates the universe and a God who enters into the almonry to bestow His alms. They would have a God who upholds the pillars of the earth, but when God would enter into His throne chair, then the world would gnash its teeth and Shake its head and fist against God. But you and I know that the only God there is, is the God who is the sovereign Lord of heaven and earth; the God who will do all of His pleasure and whose purposes shall come to pass.

If you are a Christian you can say, "Thanks be unto God that the sovereign Ruler of heaven and earth is my gracious Saviour." If you are not, then, my friend, quickly repent of your sins and turn unto Him who says, ". . . Him that cometh to me I will in no wise cast out." Receive His mercy while there is still time. For He says, "I am He that killeth and maketh alive, that woundeth and maketh whole, and there is none that can deliver out of my hand."

John 6:37

Deuteronomy 32:39

Father, may we go forth into Your world knowing that You are the sovereign Ruler of every blade of grass. From the atoms in the smallest insect, to the stars that move in their courses, You are the sovereign God. O God, may none of us be guilty of the most grievous sin of rejecting Your grace, mercy, free forgiveness, and gracious gift of life eternal given to those who trust in Christ. For indeed everyone of us shall one day come to Jesus Christ as Saviour in this world, or as Judge in that one which is to come. *Amen.*

2 DOES MAN HAVE FREE WILL?

If the Son therefore shall make you free, ye shall be free indeed.

John 8:36

Does man have free will? I think most recognize this to be one of the deepest subjects to have ever occupied the minds of the world's greatest thinkers. Theologians as well as philosophers have given themselves to this great enigma: Does man really have free will? or is he merely a puppet moved around by the forces of fate? It seems to be a contradiction that an all-sovereign God and a free creature could exist in the same universe. It would seem that if man is free then God does not control *all* things.

First of all to ask if man has a free will is to put the question in an improper form. It's more accurate to talk about a free agent or free soul because the will of man never acts independently from the rest of his faculties. Man's will isn't some sort of internal gyroscope moving and turning any way it pleases. Rather, it is an integral part of the human being—the human soul.

What is the soul of man? Man's soul consists of his intellect, emotions, and volition or, more simply, his mind, heart, and will. Therefore, when man decides or wills an action, it comes first from his mind. Then because he has some knowledge, he gets a feeling—human affections and appetites come into play.

These two then act on any given issue and tell the will what to do. The will, *without exception*, does what the mind and heart tell it to do. Man's will, therefore, never acts contrarily to his mind and heart.

The second problem with the question, "Does man have free will?" is one of semantics. What exactly do we mean by free will? Do we mean: Does he have the ability to choose whatever he *wants* to do? The answer is: Yes, he does! This is an inalienable contribution of God to the human soul —that man *always* and *only* does what he pleases. Man is a self-motivating agent. He can originate action and choose whatever he pleases on any given occasion.

Dr. John Gerstner writes that it is impossible to force the will of man. To have a forced free will would be contrary to the meaning of the word. He illustrates this by saying that if he could place a book in your hands, point a gun to your temple, and say, "You will read this book or I'll splatter your brains all over the wall!" that would still not force your will because you would then come to the place of making a decision. Your mind would feed certain facts to your consciousness, emotions, and affections as to how much you love or didn't love life. Quite likely you would come to the decision to read the book!

Under other circumstances, with things more significant than merely reading a book, there have been Christians who have come to other conclusions. In effect, Nero said to millions of Christians: "You will renounce Jesus Christ and blaspheme His name or you will wish someone would blow out your brains. You will be peeled, boiled, fed to lions, and put in sacks with snakes and vipers." Faced with such a choice, hundreds of thousands of Christians made a decision! Their minds fed them certain facts about this life and eternity and most thought it was better to lose this life and gain eternity than to gain a few more years on earth and lose eternal life. Their affections went out to Jesus Christ whom they loved more than life itself. Their decision was: "Bring on the lions!" But that was their choice! It wasn't forced! Without exception, man does whatever he pleases in light of the facts and feelings involved.

I said that man is free in every case to do whatever he pleases. But it doesn't necessarily follow that man is free to do what he *ought* to do! Now, what ought man to do? Man ought to love God, repent of his sins, by faith embrace Jesus Christ. Man ought to love the commandments of God, desire a holy life, love purity, holiness, righteousness. Man ought to strive for all these things. But the Bible makes it clear that every man is not free to do what he ought to do.

The Bible tells us that God made man—Adam and Eve —and gave them the power of contrary choice. He also gave them the ability to do that which was good, to do what they ought to. And they ought to have obeyed God and kept the commandments He gave them! Notice: They had the ability to do good as well as evil. This was man in a state of innocency, his first state, and without the experience of evil until he made that first fatal choice.

The Bible describes man's second state as being in sin. Because Adam sinned, he plunged the whole human race into sin and death in sin, which means all of us are born with his fallen nature. After first shattering and marring the image of God, Adam then brought forth creatures in his own fallen image. Some people believe man is born in the same condition as was Adam. This is not true. Adam was born in innocency; thereafter all men were born in sin.

The Bible describes man in sin as the natural man with a natural desire to sin. This doesn't mean he goes around robbing banks! This means that whatever he does is sin. The Bible says that the plowing of the wicked is sin. When he goes out and works at a job, it is sin. When he eats his dinner, it is sin because he's getting strength to continue his rebellion against God. In his natural state of sin, man's heart, emotions, mind, motives, ends, goals, everything is contrary to God.

Proverbs 21:4

The things which the natural man does may be good in themselves. He may give a million dollars to charity but does it for the wrong reasons and wrong motives—perhaps to get a deduction on his income tax or get the praise of men. Jesus said, "Ye seek the praise of men rather than the praise of God." Man often has a false idea that in some way he's going to buy himself some real estate in heaven. The Bible says: ". . . They that are in the flesh cannot please God." Therefore, it is impossible for the natural man to do good things without first knowing Christ, without first being born anew of the Spirit, redeemed.

John 12:43

Romans 8:8

The Bible also says that the natural man is at enmity against God; that he is not subject to the law of God, neither indeed can he be. The Bible says that man is dead

Romans 8:7
Ephesians 2:1, 5

John 3:19
John 8:34

in his sins; he loves unrighteousness rather than righteousness; he is bound to his sin.

The question now is: Does the natural man have the freedom to choose to do good, to choose Jesus Christ, to come to God? The answer is unequivocally: No!

Many Protestants talk about the natural man as if he had the power to simply cease being unrighteous and ungodly and start being a godly man! This was a Romanist teaching and not that of Luther or the other Reformers. One of Luther's greatest books was on *The Bondage of the Will*. It was Erasmus, the rationalist, who wrote on the *freedom* of the will. Luther said that man was bound in sin and controlled by his own passions and desires and could not cease from these to do good. Experientially, Luther knew this to be his own condition. Jesus taught the same thing. He said:

John 15:15
John 8:34

"Ye were the servants of sin. Henceforth I call you no longer servants but friends." Jesus also said: ". . . Whosoever committeth sin is the servant of sin." It's interesting to note that Martin Luther called himself Martin Eleutheros, Martin the free. He had been the bondslave of sin, shackled by his passions and desires, but he met Christ and was set free.

Jesus said: "If the Son therefore shall make you free, ye

John 8:36
John 8:32

shall be free indeed," and, ". . . Ye shall know the truth, and the truth shall make you free." The scribes and Pharisees, however, didn't like this. "We are Abraham's seed," they said. "We have never been in bondage to anyone." Then Jesus said: "He that committeth sin is the

John 8:33, 34

bondslave of sin." Iniquity and unrighteousness control the natural man's life and he does what they tell him to do. But if the Son shall make you free, ye shall be free indeed! Consider the implication of that—if the Son shall make you free, you shall be free!

In his natural state, man is a bondslave to sin. A bondslave thinks he can do whatever he wants but he always chooses to do the wrong thing. Place a Bible and a bottle before an alcoholic. He's free to do whatever he wants; the trouble is we know what he always wants! Invite a dope addict to a heroin party or a prayer meeting; he's free to do whatever he wants, but the problem is *what* he wants! Give a box of chocolates to a glutton; he's free to eat them or not—but is he really free? No! He's controlled by his appetite. He's bound and therefore the servant of his own emotions, affections, desires, and passions.

Let me point out that he could choose to eliminate any one of these things, but he could not choose to make himself holy. Because even if he got rid of his alcohol, dope, or gluttony, he would still be an unholy sinner, incapable of choosing Jesus Christ. Why is he in this condition? His mind and heart are darkened by sin. They deceive him. He is at enmity with God.

Why is it when the natural man looks at Jesus Christ, the One who is altogether lovely, that there is nothing about Him that makes him desire Him? It's because his heart and mind give him the wrong message. He chooses not to repent and yield his life to Jesus Christ. Such a man is not free. He is bound and in a *state of sin*.

However, when the natural man receives Jesus Christ into his heart as Saviour and Lord, he is regenerated, made new, and is in a *state of grace*. He is now able to do good. Because he has God's grace, he will gain victory in his life and finally come to a *state of glory*. In the state of glory (the redeemed state of man in heaven), he has been sealed by God and is now able to do only good.

The biblical teaching about man is: First, he was in the *state of innocency*—able to do good, able to sin. Second, in the *state of sin* (his fallen nature), he is able only to sin. He is unable to change his moral nature, incapable of lifting himself up into holiness. Third, in the *state of grace*, he can do both. And fourth, in the *state of glory*, he will be sealed to do only that which is good.

If you've never received Jesus Christ, then I urge you to examine yourself and see your utter helplessness; your total inability to suppose yourself to do anything but that which is displeasing to God. May you be enabled by His grace to cry out to the Son of Glory to set you free—that you may be free indeed!

> Long my imprisoned spirit lay
> Fast bound in sin and nature's night.
> Thine eye diffused a quick'ning ray;
> I woke—the dungeon flamed with light!
> My chains fell off, my heart was free,
> I rose, went forth, and followed thee.
> **CHARLES WESLEY**

Lord Jesus, we thank You that You have made those that trust in You free. That You have made us kings and heirs of Your Kingdom. That You have delivered us from the bondage of sin and declared that sin shall no longer have dominion over us. Father, I pray for those who are still in the bondage of their own making. A bondage which ties, binds, and draws them downward ever into deeper sin. I pray, Father, that You will deliver them from these shackles and set the prisoners free. May they come out of their bondage, darkness, and sin to the One who can make them free—to Christ, the great Emancipator from sin. *Amen.*

3 PREDESTINATION

*And we know that all things work together for good to them that
love God, to them who are the called according to his purpose.
For whom he did foreknow, he also did predestinate to be
conformed to the image of his Son, that he might be the firstborn
among many brethren. Moreover whom he did predestinate,
them he also called: and whom he called, them he also justified:
and whom he justified, them he also glorified.*

Romans 8:28–30

I had a brief discourse with a friend recently during
which I mentioned predestination. This prompted an out-
burst concerning why the doctrine of predestination was
contrary to all manner of Christian principles, ethics, and
motives. Unfortunately, I did not have time to discuss the
matter further with the gentleman, but I think he is typical
of many people today, both in and out of the church, who
would find the doctrine of predestination to be somewhat
alien. You would think that one were a setter-forth of
strange doctrines, as the Apostle Paul was accused of
being, when you mention the doctrine of
predestination—as if this were something totally foreign
and alien to Christianity. Truly this doctrine has fallen on
bad times in our day.

Why is this? The great A. A. Hodge, professor at Princeton, said that this is due, in a large measure, to the inatten-

tion which is paid to it in the churches, and to the general prevalence of a natural, though unfounded and ignorant prejudice against it. I think it is true that there is a natural prejudice on the part of men against this doctrine as there is to all of the doctrines of grace and at this point, the sovereign grace of God reaches its apex and therefore that prejudice becomes most obvious here.

B. B. Warfield, also at Princeton, said in answer to the question why man in this particular time is so opposed to this doctrine: "Consider the pride of man, his assertion of freedom, his boast of power, his refusal to acknowledge the sway of any other's will. Consider the ingrained confidence of the sinner in his own fundamentally good nature." How true this is. As I have talked to thousands of people, I find that most all of them are basically convinced that at their heart and in their core, they are basically good. Well, that wasn't what Jesus said about the heart, was it? Some of these people say, "Oh, I believe that Jesus is the Master Teacher." Jesus said, "For out of the heart proceed evil thoughts, murders, adulteries, fornications, thefts, false

Matthew 15:19

witness, blasphemies," and that we are, everyone of us, sinners in our hearts. The Bible says, "The heart is deceitful above all things, and desperately wicked: who can know it?

Jeremiah 17:9, 10

I the Lord search the heart . . . ." Yet the unregenerate man, the non-Christian man, has an ingrained confidence in his fundamentally good nature. There is no such thing, we are told, as a bad boy. Well, how many times have we heard that? But that is not what the Scripture says. The Scripture says, "There is none that doeth good, no, not

Psalms 53:3

one"—either boy or man, girl or woman, Christian or non-Christian—there is none good, no, not one. The whole class has flunked because of man's ingrained confidence in his own fundamentally good nature and his confidence in his full ability to perform all that can be justly demanded of him. Warfield says that particularly at this time, when man, through science, has made such spectacular advances in his power over nature and is so filled with pride of accomplishment that he finds it particularly difficult to humble himself beneath the mighty hand of God. He must come to the place of realizing that he is not only guilty and polluted, but absolutely helpless and hopeless. There is nothing he can do to prepare himself, for his salvation is entirely in the hands of God. That is why Dr. L. Boettner says that it is almost totally impossible to convince the unregenerate heart of this doctrine. Let me say that again: It is almost totally impossible to convince the unregenerate heart (the unsaved man, the unbeliever) of this doctrine. The natural man, in his natural unregenerate state, rises up in revolt against it. And so being the pinnacle of sovereign grace, it is a touchstone by which men's characters are revealed, as whether or not they are truly submissive to Christ and His Word. In studying it, your heart will be revealed to you this hour. You will never be the same. Some of you will hate the thought of predestination; some will love and cherish it. But keep in mind, it is practically impossible to convince the unregenerate mind of this doctrine.

That this should be looked upon as an alien doctrine today is even stranger when we take a brief historical review. This doctrine was set forth very plainly in the early church by St. Augustine, so much that it held sway over the church for most of the early centuries until the church finally sank into apostasy. It was revived again by Martin Luther, who was a firm believer in the doctrine of predestination. John Calvin of Geneva was also a firm believer and set it forth with such cogency and power that it even has taken on his name in some circles as if he had invented it, which of course is far from the truth. He simply stated it with great clarity. It was held also by Melanchthon, by Zwingli, by John Knox, and by Cranmer in England. All, without exception, of the Reformers of the Protestant Reformation were firm believers in the doctrine of predestination. It was, says Hastings, the historian, "the very Hercules might of the Protestant Reformation whereby the Reformers took the salvation of the human soul out of the hands of the pope and put it firmly in the hands of God. Now is it not strange that the descendants of these Reformers, who claim to believe their doctrines, so frequently vehemently deny this which they held to be a cardinal teaching of the Scriptures. All Protestant churches which came into being out of the Reformation hold to that doctrine in their creeds. The most moral people that the world has ever seen have been believers in this doctrine. The Presbyterians and the Reformed of Holland and Switzerland and Germany, the Anglicans, the Huguenots, the Covenanters, the Puritans, the Pietists of Germany, the Pilgrims of America, were all firm believers in this great doctrine of predestination.

The makers of civil liberty, such as John Calvin; the

virtual founder of democracy, William of Orange; Cromwell; and the Presbyterian and Congregational founders of the government of this nation were all believers in this great doctrine. Pioneer provisions for universal education sprang from the Scottish parochial school which was built upon this doctrine. The New England College was founded upon this great teaching as well. Dr. L. Boettner said that the patriots, free-state makers, martyrs, and missionaries of the modern era have been overwhelmingly believers in the doctrine of predestination.

Therefore, I would have you reconsider whatever prejudice you may have against this doctrine in the light of some of these facts of history. What I would urge would be a calm, careful study of the matter. I am sure that what you will obtain in one chapter like this would not be sufficient and I would urge you to make a further study of it. There are many books dealing with the subject. I would encourage you to study them. Adapting the words of Alexander Pope we might say that a little predestination is a dangerous thing, so drink deeply from the sacred spring or drink not at all.

The reason people today are opposed to it is because they will have God to be anything but God. He can be a cosmic psychiatrist, a helpful shepherd, a leader, a teacher, anything at all . . . only not God. For a very simple reason —they want to be God themselves. This has always been the essence of sin—that man wants to be God. From the very time that Lucifer said, "I will be like unto God." So Adam said unto God, "God, you keep your hands off my life. I'm going to run it my way." Oh, it's not that we desire so much to bind the influences of the Pleiades or manipulate Orion, it's that we want to be the God of our own lives. We want to be the captains of our fates and the masters of our souls. This mastery we do not want to give up to God or anyone else.

But what about the Scriptures? I am tempted to ask sometimes of people who say they do not believe in this doctrine, "Do you believe in the Bible?" One unquestionable thing is that the Scriptures are filled with this teaching. Simply to write out the passages in the Scripture that deal with predestination, election, the efficacious calling of God's spirit of people unto salvation, foreordination, God's sovereignty over all phases of the world, would take more space than we have in this entire chapter. That you might

Isaiah 14:13

Genesis 3

see that this doctrine is plainly taught in the Scripture, let us look at a few. That there are a group of people in the Bible known as the *elect*—those that are chosen of God—is clear from such passages as these: ". . . Except those days [the last days] should be shortened, there should no flesh be saved: but for the elect's sake those days shall be shortened . . . . For there shall arise false Christs, and false prophets, and shall shew great signs and wonders; insomuch that, if it were possible, they shall deceive the very elect . . . . And [God] shall send his angels with a great sound of a trumpet, and they shall gather together his elect from the four winds . . . . Who shall lay any thing to the charge of God's elect? It is God that justifieth. Who is he that condemneth?" Christ said that we should rejoice, because our names are written in the Lamb's book of life, written from the foundation of the earth. Said Paul, "Therefore I endure all things for the elect's sake . . . ." "Paul, a servant of God, and an apostle of Jesus Christ, according to the faith of God's elect." "Knowing, brethren beloved, your election of God." We can know that we are elect. If we have come to Christ and have been regenerated and redeemed, we may know that we are elect because we would never come otherwise.

Matthew 24:22

Matthew 24:24

Matthew 24:31

Romans 8:33, 34

Luke 10:20
Revelation 21:27

2 Timothy 2:10

Titus 1:1
1 Thessalonians 1:4

Also we read of "having predestinated us unto the adoption of children by Jesus Christ to himself, according to the good pleasure of his will . . . . In whom also we have obtained an inheritance, being predestinated according to the purpose of him who worketh all things after the counsel of his own will."

Ephesians 1:5, 11

Romans tells us that "Moreover whom he did predestinate, them he also called: and whom he called, them he also justified: and whom he justified, them he also glorified." We see the "Golden Chain" that takes our salvation from eternity past to eternity future and is bound up in the predestinating love and will of God.

Romans 8:30

When Jesus had gone into Bethsaida, Capernaum, and to various towns and preached and His preaching had been rejected, what did He do? He sat down by the edge of the road and said, "Oh, Father, I'm so miserable! They have all rejected my preaching. I did the best I could but they just wouldn't hearken unto me. They just wouldn't respond! Oh, Lord, I surely wish that they would respond. I'm so sad." Is that what He did? Read His words in Matthew 11. Jesus at that time lifted up His eyes to heaven and said, "I thank thee, O Father, Lord of heaven and earth, because thou hast hid these things from the wise and prudent, and hast revealed them unto babes." Why? Why has God done this? "Even so, Father: for so it seemeth good in thy sight."

Matthew 11:25
Matthew 11:26

Now, since this is just a sampling of many, many passages which mention this doctrine, what does it actually mean? What is it saying? Charles Spurgeon, considered by many to be the most famous and outstanding preacher of all times, said that in a world of fallen men, where all of them have rebelled against God and gone the way of their own sin, have turned their backs upon Him, where none will seek after God, for there is none that seeketh after God, no, not one, what good is a *whosoever will* in a world where *everybody won't?* Man inevitably refuses to come to God. Though God would extend His arms all day long, "All day long I have stretched forth my hands unto a disobedient and gainsaying people," saying, "Why will ye not come? Why will ye die? And you would not."

Romans 10:21
John 5:40

There are only two things anyone is going to get from God: one is justice. God must be just with everyone. "The judge of the earth must do rightly." It is incumbent upon God to be just to everyone. He cannot be unfair or unjust.

Psalms 98:9

The other thing that we can get is mercy or grace. Someone said to me one time, "Well, that's not fair." They were right! It isn't! Salvation isn't fair. If you have not learned that by now, you haven't learned much of anything about Christianity. It isn't fair. Fair means just and just means you get exactly what you deserve depending upon what you have done in light of what you have known. If we get what we deserve depending upon what we've done, we are going to get it right in the neck, because we've all done wrong. Thank God that grace is not fair!

Now it is not unfair in the sense that it is below fair. But it is super*fair*, it is mercy, it is beyond and above fairness. If you sell a piece of property to someone that is worth a thousand dollars and they cheat you and only give you five hundred dollars, that is not fair. But suppose they give you five hundred thousand dollars for a piece of property which is evidently worth only a thousand, that is not fair; that is better than fair. Grace is better than fair.

Romans 9:15

God doesn't have to give grace or mercy to anyone. He said, "I will have mercy on whom I will have mercy . . . ." When a governor forgives or pardons some criminal in the penitentiary, it doesn't mean that he has to pardon every criminal in every penitentiary in the state. That is an executive privilege of a sovereign. He may extend it or withhold it as he sees fit. God looks down upon a fallen world and He decides to extend mercy; and to freely forgive a person who condignly deserves to be punished for his sins. Therefore God extends to that person mercy. Charles Spurgeon asked if there was anything wrong with that. And so I ask you, is there anything wrong with God extending mercy and freely pardoning and forgiving someone who doesn't deserve it at all? "Is it not lawful for me to do what I will with mine own?" said Christ when He extended mercy to someone. No, there is nothing wrong with that. According to Spurgeon, then is it not all right that God should *decide* to do that yesterday and then *do* it today? Or decide to do it last week and then do it today? Or last month or year or century or before the foundation of the world? And that, my friends, is election or predestination. That God looked down from all eternity upon a world of sinners and decided to extend mercy to a vast number of people whom no man can number and in their appointed time He extended that mercy, not because of anything foreseen in them but entirely and totally because of what God was . . . the God of all grace. So much for the statement of the doctrine.

Matthew 20:15

There have been many objections which have been raised against this. One is, "Well, why doesn't God save everyone?" There are some things which are revealed and the things which are revealed belong unto the children of men and the things which are not revealed, belong unto God. God has not been pleased to reveal to us everything. He has not revealed to us fully why He has not chosen everyone. But it is for reasons which seem good in His sight. Why did Jesus say that He had withheld this grace? Notice His words again: "I thank thee, O Father, Lord of heaven and earth, that thou hast hid these things from the wise and prudent, and hast revealed them unto babes." Why? Notice: "Even so, Father; for so it seemed good in thy sight." Some of you won't like that. This is the place where you find whether or not you are willing to be submissive to God—not to an arbitrary pagan deity but to a God infinitely wise, infinitely gracious, infinitely just, infinitely holy. For reasons which seem good unto Him, He has extended grace to some and withheld it from others.

Deuteronomy 29:29

Luke 10:21

There are some clues that the Bible gives us. One thing

we can know—what is *not* the reason why it is extended to those of us to whom it has been extended. He didn't extend it to us because we are better than anyone else, nor nobler than anyone else, wiser or smarter or holier than anyone else. Rather, the Bible says in 1 Corinthians, chapter 1, "For ye see your calling, brethren, how that not many wise men after the flesh, not many mighty, not many noble, are called: But God hath chosen the foolish things of the world to confound the wise; and God hath chosen the weak things of the world to confound the things which are mighty; And base things of the world, and things which are despised, hath God chosen, yea, and things which are not, to bring to nought things that are: That no flesh should glory in his presence." So the fact, that I know that I am one of God's elect, gives me no grounds for boasting, because God specifically tells me that He has chosen the junk of this world. There is no place for boasting. "That no flesh should glory in his presence. He that glorieth, let him glory in the Lord."

1 Corinthians 1:26–29

1 Corinthians 1:29
1 Corinthians 1:31

Salvation is not by works or human merit lest anyone should boast. We have nothing to boast about. We also may derive from the Scripture this realization: that God has created the world for His own glory and not simply for our pleasure. That God is glorified because He is a glorious Being and the many facets of God's character, like a magnificent diamond, are glorious and to be glorified they simply must be seen. Thus in the salvation of the redeemed the glorious aspects of God's mercy, His grace, His compassion, His long-suffering, His kindness, and His love are revealed and God is glorified. But in the just condemnation of the wicked, the glorious aspects of God's justice, holiness, and righteousness are manifested, and God is also glorified. Now for us, who see all of this with the jaundiced eyes of sinners, we find that hard to see. But an angel, who is without sin, would find no difficulty with it at all. God is just and holy and righteous and has a natural indignation and hatred of sin, because sin is inherently evil. When these qualities are manifested in the just condemnation of sinners, God, in His justice, is glorified in the same way that a judge is glorified when he justly condemns a wicked criminal. Therefore, both in the electing of some and the passing by of others, God is glorified.

Others have raised this objection: "Why, this is fatalism!" This simply reveals how little they know about predestination or how little they know about fatalism. If they understood both of these properly they would know that predestination is the only genuine alternative that there is to fatalism. This is very important. Fatalism allows no place for any sort of freedom for man. Where the Bible teaches that the natural, unsaved, unregenerate man is dead and bound in his sins and therefore cannot do the things that he *ought,* such as repenting and living a holy life, it also teaches that all men whether in the state of innocency, sin, grace, or glory, are always free to do what they *want.* Let me state that again. Though man in his natural, unregenerate state is bound in sin and cannot do what he *ought,* all men are always free to do what they *want.* Because they are free to do whatever they *please,* they are responsible for whatever they *do.* Therefore, the liberty and contingency of second causes are maintained and not destroyed as they are in fatalism.

Some people suppose that by accepting the doctrine of chance they will avoid this problem. But all you have to do is read cursorily in the philosophy of science to know that chance is absolutely deterministic. The only difference between chance and fatalism is that in *fatalism* you are held by some impersonal force that controls everything; in *chance,* you are given over into the hands of some sort of impersonal machine which is either going to chop you up or bring you out on top, but is an impersonal, unthinking force. Whereas, the Bible would put us into the hands of an all-knowing, all-loving Father, a personal Being. There is a vast gulf of difference between fatalism and predestination. This is even more obvious as Jesus said, ". . . for the tree is known by his fruit." Look at the Muslim world where fatalism has been its teaching for thirteen hundred years. There you see nations which have been plunged into stagnation and poverty. Then look to the lands of the doctrine of predestination—Switzerland, Holland, Germany, England, Scotland, America—and you see nations that have had the greatest of progress. The difference is so obvious that the most cursory examination would reveal it.

It is also objected that predestination destroys any sort of motivation. This is because people have the idea that in order to be motivated to do anything, what is done must be unknown and uncertain. But this is not true and a little reflection will show that regardless of what you believe about predestination, if you believe in God at all, you believe in an Omniscient Being who knows all things.

Ezekiel 24:14

Acts 26:18

Matthew 12:33

"Known unto God are all his works from the beginning of the world," the Scripture says. God knows everything. Now, if you have a God that simply *knows* everything, that knowledge renders every future event certain. May I point out why? A hundred million years ago, did God know that you would be reading this book at this hour? You say, "Of course, God knew everything." He knew that a hundred million years ago. If you don't believe that, you don't believe in God. Everybody who believes in God knows that one of the attributes of God is omniscience. If God didn't know that and He just learned it today because He saw you here, then God just learned something and thus God would not be immutable or unchangeable. He would have just changed; He just grew in His knowledge. Thus He is destroyed as God. If God, a hundred million years ago knew that you were going to be reading this book at this hour, is there any possibility that you would not now be reading it? Of course not! His knowledge rendered that fact absolutely certain. You know that. At the same time, you know that you picked up this book by your own free will, because you are free to do what you please to do. Now this is a mystery we cannot comprehend, how God has ordained all things to work together as men please and yet God overrules and works everything according to His good pleasure. "For it is God that worketh in you both to will and

Philippians 2:13   to do of his good pleasure."

So you see that regardless of what you believe about predestination—if you simply believe in God, an omniscient God, every future act is rendered certain. But the fact that something is certain doesn't mean that you are not free. That God will always act in a righteous manner is absolutely certain. There is no question about that. He cannot act in any other way, and yet there is no being so free as God. So, therefore, the doctrine of predestination, because it renders future events certain, does not take away the liberty of secondary causes; nor does it mean that people are not free to do what they want.

Some people say, "Why should I pray?" For example, when you pray that God would convert some non-Christian friend or relative, are you not praying that God would do the very thing that we are talking about? If God can't do this, if God cannot convert people, if it is not God who saves people, if all we can do is present facts and hope that people will respond, then there is no sense in really praying to God at all. One of the first rules of salesmanship is to go to the person who has the power to make the decision. So quit getting on your knees to God and go kneel down before the man and pray to him to be saved. He has the final decision, if you don't believe in predestination. But we pray always as if God had the ability to convert the soul just as He did the Apostle Paul.

Acts 9:1–20

"Why should we witness and why should we preach?" The reason people ask this is because they do not understand that God doesn't foreordain simply the *ends,* but He also foreordains the *means. God does not foreordain the ends without also foreordaining the means.* If He has foreordained that somebody would be converted, He has also foreordained that somebody would share the Gospel and would pray for him. That person in turn would have been converted prior to that—the continuous praying and converting would have reached all the way back to the beginning of the world. God never foreordains ends without also foreordaining means.

The doctrine of election is full of great consolation and there are very great practical benefits to holding it and understanding it. The thirty-nine articles of the Church of England, in its seventeenth article says, ". . . the godly consideration of Predestination, and our Election in Christ, is full of sweet, pleasant, and unspeakable comfort to godly persons . . . ." Notice, that "to godly persons" but if you are not godly, it is not full of comfort to you. It is full of comfort because it shows that salvation is all of grace. Keep in mind that the Bible never says that anyone is predestined to hell. The word is only used of heaven, grace, and glory. But you say, "If God predestinates some to heaven, and if He passes by others, isn't He predestinating them to hell?" No, that is not the case, because this supposes that these people are neutral and are not going any place by themselves. The whole world is rushing headlong into wickedness, sin, and thus into condemnation and hell.

Here are five people who are planning to hold up a bank. They are friends of mine. I find out about it and I plead with them. I beg them not to do it. Finally they push me out of the way and they start out. I tackle one of the men and wrestle him to the ground. The others go ahead, rob the bank, a guard is killed, they are captured, convicted, sentenced to the electric chair, and die. The one man who was not involved in the robbery goes free. Now I ask you this question: Whose fault was it that these other men died? Did I make them hold up the bank? Did I encourage them to do it? Did I cause them to do it? Did I urge them to do it? Or did I not plead with them not to do it? Was it not their own free choice of their own sinful hearts, their own cupidity, their own lust for money, that caused them to do it? They had nobody to blame but themselves. Now this other man who is walking around free—can he say, "Because my heart is so good, I am a free man"? The only reason that he is free is because of me; because I restrained him. So those who go to hell *have no one to blame but themselves.* Those who go to heaven *have no one to praise but Jesus Christ.* Thus we see that salvation is *all of grace,* from its beginning to its end. It is all of God. He is the one that seeks us and draws us unto Himself.

This doctrine gives great security and courage to those who believe it. For those for whom God is far away and may only now and then be involved in the activities of this life, life is full of fear and danger. But those that live and move in God and know that He sovereignly controls every atom of this universe, these people are filled with good courage and confidence. Predestination extinguishes fear and it is interesting to note that those who held to it were afraid of no one. It brings men low before God but it lifts Him high and makes them strong before kings. Thus Mary Queen of Scots could say that she feared the face of John Knox more than ten thousand ships.

Do you know, beloved, your election in Christ? The Bible says, ". . . make your calling and election sure." Christ is inviting you to come. ". . . him that cometh to me I will in no wise cast out." Predestination keeps no one out of heaven, but it populates paradise with a vast multitude of people that no man can number. Christ says, ". . . come to me; and him that cometh to me, I will in no wise cast out." But of yourself, you will never come. ". . . there is none that seeketh after God. No, not one." If you do *not* come to Christ and trust His cross and cease to trust in your own righteousness, and put your trust in His atoning work, you have nothing to blame but the self-righteousness, pride, and love of sin in your own heart. It you do come to Christ, it will be because God, the great and gracious Shepherd has sought you out and brought you to Himself.

The lost sheep does not find the shepherd; the shepherd
finds the lost sheep.

> Hark! 'tis the Shepherd's voice I hear,
> Out in the desert dark and drear,
> Calling the sheep who've gone a-stray
> Far from the Shepherd's fold away.

Soli Deo Gloria!

4 EFFECTUAL CALLING

Moreover whom he did predestinate, them he also called: and whom he called, them he also justified: and whom he justified, them he also glorified.

Romans 8:30

In the first three chapters, we have seen that God is the sovereign Ruler of the world; He does not work helter-skelter, nor does He ad-lib as He goes along day-by-day. Rather He laid the architectural plans for all His works before He created the world. He sovereignly controls and ordains all things which come to pass, from the greatest star to the smallest atom.

We have seen that He has done this in such a way as to leave a certain natural liberty to man. He created man with a power to do good or evil. But man chose evil and plunged the world into sin, bringing himself into a state of bondage, condemnation. We find God determined not to leave him there but from all eternity selected a people for Himself. The Scriptures refer to these as His elect, His chosen ones—a multitude of every tongue, kindred, nation, and tribe under the sun; a multitude no man can number. These God determined to save. These are His sheep, the predestinated ones for whom Paul bore all things and for whom the days of tribulation will be shortened. These are the ones who will hear and understand His voice and will

Mark 13:20, 27

43

follow Him because they know God sent His Son to die and procure eternal life for them.

In this chapter, I want to consider how this redemption, which has been procured by Christ and chosen by God, is to be applied. This doctrine is called "Effectual Calling." Most know what a calling is, but what is an effectual calling? *Effectual* means that which effectuates whatever it attempts to do. It is that which works, is successful, and succeeds in doing that which the author intends. This is what God means when He says: "[And] my word . . . shall not return unto me void, but it shall accomplish *that which I please,* and it shall prosper *in the thing whereto I sent it.*" What purpose shall it accomplish? Shall it accomplish the purpose of the people that hear it? No, it shall accomplish the purpose for which God sent it. It is effectual to do His work.

Isaiah 55:11

The Bible speaks of both a calling which is effectual and a calling which is not. There is the outer calling which is merely the Word unaccompanied by the Holy Spirit. When I say in the name of Jesus Christ that He declares, "Come unto me and I will give you life," that's an outward, external calling by the Word. If someone should respond to that calling, they would receive eternal life because God will refuse no one. ". . . Him that cometh to me I will in no wise cast out."

Matthew 25:34

John 6:37

But there is a problem. Man in his fallen condition (natural, unregenerate man) is so bound by sin and blinded by his iniquity that he desires to have nothing to do with the holy God because his heart is at enmity with God. "There is none that understandeth, there is none that seeketh after God." Every person who seeks after God will find Him. "And ye shall seek me, and find me, when ye shall search for me with all your heart." But there is none that seeketh after God. Why? "But the natural man receiveth not the things of the Spirit of God: for they are foolishness unto him: neither can he know them, because they are spiritually discerned." The problem is man's will which is set against God and bound in its own sin.

Romans 3:11

Jeremiah 29:13

1 Corinthians 2:14

Therefore, before a person comes to Christ there must be something more than an external invitation. There must be an inward work of the Spirit of God who effectually woos and draws us to Christ so we come freely, being made willing by His grace. The ineffectual calling (the outward call) is seen in Matthew 22:14: "For many are called [by the gospel every week] but few are chosen." Keep in mind the few is a multitude no man can number, but few compared to the vast billions of people who have lived upon earth.

Matthew 22:14

The effectual or inward call is seen in Romans 8:30: ". . . Whom he did predestinate, them he also called: and whom he called, them he also justified . . . ." Those he called, came! Unquestionably, all God's elect shall come unto Him. "As many as the Father giveth me *shall come* to me . . . ." All those the Father has given unto the Son as a reward for His suffering and passion, they will come unto Him and He shall see His seed and be satisfied. So there is both an outward and an inward call.

Romans 8:30

John 6:37

Isaiah 53:11

This doctrine of effectual calling is also called *irresistible* or *efficacious grace*. The following is a succinct statement of this doctrine as contained in the Westminster Confession of Faith, which is the doctrinal standard of the Reformed world:

All of those whom God hath predestinated unto life, and those only, He is pleased, in His appointed and accepted time, effectually to call, by His Word and Spirit, out of that state of sin and death in which they are by nature, to grace and salvation by Jesus Christ: enlightening their minds, spiritually and savingly, to understand the things of God, taking away their heart of stone, and giving unto them an heart of flesh, renewing their wills, and by His almighty power determining them to that which is good; and effectually drawing them to Jesus Christ; yet so as they come most freely, being made willing by His grace. This effectual call is of God's free and special grace alone, not from anything at all foreseen in man, who is altogether passive therein, until, being quickened and renewed by the Holy Spirit, he is thereby enabled to answer this call, and to embrace the grace offered and conveyed in it.

This then is effectual calling. The agent is the Holy Spirit; the instrument is the Word of God; the objects of the call are unregenerate sinners, specifically those of God's elect.

In 2 Thessalonians 2:13, 14 we read: ". . . God hath from the beginning chosen you to salvation . . . . Whereunto he called you by our gospel, to the obtaining of the glory of our Lord Jesus Christ." And there you have the picture. Before the beginning of the world, God chose them, and having chosen them, He determined to see they received the gift of eternal life. He is going to bring it to pass in His appointed time. The Spirit will call them by

2 Thessalonians 2:13, 14

the gospel unto Christ and they will receive that which God has given them.

Of course, there are many people who don't begin to understand the rudiments of Christianity and suppose salvation is something earned by their own good works. But salvation is a gift—unearned, unmerited, and undeserved. It is a gift given purely by the grace and goodness of God. Now the question is: How does He give this gift? We look around and see people who hear the gospel and embrace Jesus Christ while others do not. Those who accept Jesus Christ into their lives are puzzled why others who have heard the same gospel do not.

There are two schools of thought, or two theological systems within Protestantism, which attempt to answer this question. The first is Calvinism which is espoused by the Presbyterian Church and many others. The second is Arminianism—both named after two theologians, John Calvin and Jacob Arminius. The Arminian says: "The difference is to be found in man." The Calvinist says: "The difference is to be found in God," and quotes the following Scripture to support his view: "For who maketh thee to differ from another? and what hast thou that thou didst not receive?" What causes you to differ? Yourself? What do you have that you did not receive? Do you have faith? Where did you get it? Do you have repentance? Where did you get it? Do you love God? Whence is that love? All springs from the fountain of God.

1 Corinthians 4:7

But the Arminian system says God offers eternal life to everyone, and some will believe and accept it; others will not. If this were true, then a person could say, "I have heard the gospel; I believe and accept Christ, therefore, I have eternal life. And you, my neighbor, have heard the same gospel but because of your sinful and hard heart you've turned your back and rejected it. Therefore, you are not saved and I am." The difference is to be found in us! In a sense the person is saying, "I am better than you—more spiritual, more religious, more softhearted, less in love with sin and the world. Therefore I will cling tenaciously to something in which I can boast. If I cannot boast of my good works, I shall at least boast of my faith." The Bible says: "But he that glorieth, let him glory in the Lord."

2 Corinthians 10:17

The two basic problems with the Arminian view are found in the nature of God and the nature of man. Most people do not understand the biblical picture of the nature of man. After the Fall, man died spiritually and remained in a condition from which nothing but the almighty power of God could deliver him. But people, failing to understand this, suppose man can free himself from his trespasses and sin. But Jesus said to the Pharisees: "If the Son therefore shall make you free, ye shall be free indeed," which is to say that before He performs this gracious act for them, they were not free indeed. Over and over the Bible says (concerning the natural man): "Who can bring a clean thing out of an unclean? not one." But some people believe man's will is strong enough to bring a clean life, a good life, a holy act of faith, out of an unclean man. Romans 5:12 says: "Wherefore, as by one man sin entered into the world, and death by sin; and so death passed upon all men, for that all have sinned." Man is dead in his trespasses and sins!

John 8:36

Job 14:4

Romans 5:12

"Can the Ethiopian change his skin, or the leopard his spots? then may ye also do good, that are accustomed to do evil. "Behold, I was shapen in iniquity; and in sin did my mother conceive me." "As it is written, There is none righteous, no, not one. There is none that understandeth, there is none that seeketh after God." If the gospel consisted of no more than an invitation, then heaven indeed would be an empty place. As Spurgeon said, "What good is a 'whosoever will' in a world where everybody won't!"

So the first problem with the Arminian view is that man is not free to do what he ought. Let me make this clear: Man is always free to do what he *wants*; that's why he's responsible for everything he does. But he doesn't have the power to do what he *ought*. He ought to love God with all his heart, strength, mind, and soul, but he cannot change his character any more than the Ethiopian can change his skin or the leopard his spots. No, he is bound in his sins and, until Christ breaks the shackles and sets the prisoner free, he will remain forever bound in his own sin.

The second problem with the Arminian viewpoint is the problem of God. They say that God offers all men the choice of eternal life; therefore, it's up to man to decide whether he chooses it or not. God, they say, is trying desperately to save everybody in the world, but it's up to man to determine whether or not he's going to let Him. They picture God as saying: "It is My will that everybody in the world should be saved. But, alas, in the end I must say not My will but thine be done. For thou, O man, art the sovereign lord of this world, not I!" This is the humanist viewpoint and he likes it because it elevates his own will.

Some people suppose, because God says He would that all men should be saved and is not willing that any should perish, He's actively trying to save everybody in the world. This, I think, is a false view. If God were actively trying to do something and was prevented from doing it, then He is not God.

It is also false from the multiple statements of Scripture which state God is absolutely sovereign over all things, including the spirit, will, and heart of man. The Bible says He doeth all of His pleasure among the armies of heaven and the inhabitants of earth; He stretcheth forth His hand and there is none that can say unto Him, "What doeth thou?" or turn His hand back. As Romans 9:19 says: "For who hath resisted his will?" The answer to that is nobody—no one has ever resisted the will of God. The Bible says that He will perform all of His purpose and that not one purpose of His will be restrained.

Do we have a God who is desperately trying to save everybody and is equally failing; or do we have a God who has set His purpose and fixed His heart upon His own people, His elect, whom He hath chosen before the foundation of the world? The sovereign Lord God of heaven and earth is unfailingly bringing everyone of them into glory!

Who is the God you worship? God could be equally just and merciful if He never saved anyone. Spurgeon said that the amazing thing is not that everybody is not saved, but that anybody is saved. There is the marvel of God's grace —the general benevolence of God; He isn't willing people into perdition or causing them to be lost—their own hearts are. God's general pleasure and favor are that He is willing for all to come. He says, "I take no pleasure in the death of the wicked. Why will ye die?" But God's secret purpose is to save those whom He hath ordained from the foundation of the world. All these shall be saved. "Moreover *whom* he did predestinate, *them* he also called: and *whom* he called, *them* he also justified: and *whom* he justified, *them* he also glorified." So it is God the Holy Spirit who does the calling.

Remember, it is the Word of God that is the creative force of this world. Consider the physical universe for a moment. From where does the physical universe come? "In the

Ephesians 1:9

Romans 9:19

Ezekiel 33:11

Romans 8:30

beginning . . . . God said, Let there be light," and a multitude of galaxies leaped into existence, flaming in the sky. By the Word of God, the worlds which we see began.

Genesis 1:1, 3

Consider Lazarus. Jesus said to him: "Lazarus, come forth." But Lazarus was dead; he couldn't hear Him. If Jesus had no more than an invitation to give to him, He could have knocked at that tombstone door forever. But Christ spoke the life-giving Word and that Word brought Lazarus to life and caused his heart to beat and his lungs to work. Lazarus heard the voice of his Master and said in effect, "My beloved calls. I will go," having been made willing by His grace.

John 11:43

Consider the matter of your own physical birth. What did you have to do with it? This is a perfect example of the absolute sovereignty of God; you were not consulted in the matter! No one said, "Do you want to be sir or madam? Would you like to have black hair, blond, or perhaps no hair at all? Would you like your eyes to be brown or blue? Would you like to have white or black skin, or would red, or yellow suit you better? And where would you like to live? In Fort Lauderdale, Hong Kong, or maybe in Zaire?" Nothing of the sort! You were not consulted at all. The sovereign Lord God of heaven and earth brought you into existence without so much as a how-do-you-feel-about-it!

So it is true of our spiritual birth. God didn't consult us. God brings us to life by His own sovereign power. What is necessary for man to be reborn? Two things: God's Spirit and God's Word. That is what Jesus meant when he talked to Nicodemus. He said that a man must be born of water and the Spirit. Water, in Scripture, is a frequent illusion to the Word of God. "Ye are clean through the Word which I have spoken unto you."

John 3:5

John 15:3

It is necessary to have the outward calling of the Word. That Word is accompanied by the inward calling of the Holy Spirit who takes the Gospel of Jesus Christ and makes it a life-creating force that quickens the dead sinner from his death in sin and brings him to life in Christ. The Holy Spirit takes away his darkened mind, illumines his understanding, unstops his ears, takes away his heart of stone, gives him a heart of flesh and renews his dead will. After hearing the invitation, the sinner says, "I will come to Thee, O Christ." Afterward he *knows* it was Christ who brought him to Himself.

But what of those who are not effectually called? They

John 6:37

John 2:32

hear the outward call. May I say to you again, the Word of Christ is explicit: ". . . Him that cometh to me I will in no wise cast out." You see, I can say that to you, but I know that, unless the Spirit of God comes to you and changes your whole nature, you'll never come, and for one reason: You don't want to come! Would you like to know if you are one of God's elect? Come to Christ and you will know you are because you never would have come otherwise. "Whosoever shall call upon the name of the Lord shall be saved." When you do that you'll know it was the Spirit of God who drew you to Himself. There is a poem that puts it thus:

> I sought the Lord, and afterward I knew
>   He moved my soul to seek Him, seeking me;
> It was not I that found, O Saviour true,
>   No, I was found of Thee.
>
> AUTHOR UNKNOWN

It is not the lost sheep that finds the Shepherd!

5 THE INCOMPARABLE CHRIST

Wherefore God also hath highly exalted him, and given him a name which is above every name: That at the name of Jesus every knee should bow, of things in heaven, and things in earth, and things under the earth; And that every tongue should confess that Jesus Christ is Lord, to the glory of God the Father.

Philippians 2:9-11

Returning from a conference by plane, I found myself seated next to a young man who was a televison director from Boston. As time went on, our conversation turned to the subject of religion. He mentioned the fact that he believed himself to be a Christian; that he believed in Jesus Christ, and then he said, "However, of course, that does not mean that I do not also believe all of the other religions are good and valid and that all the other founders of these religions are also great men. Of course, I do not go along with the idea that Jesus is the 'only way.' "

That brought to my mind the question so many people ask today, "Is Christ really the only way?" Is He the incomparable Christ? Is there no one with whom He can truthfully be compared? Is He without a peer? Is He unique? Is He indeed *THE WAY, THE TRUTH, and THE LIFE* or merely a way, a truth, and a life? We might consider the

John 14:6

51

incomparable Christ and perhaps take a note from adver-
tisers who advise us to compare and determine which is the
best in everything from Cadillacs on down. Let us compare
Jesus Christ and what He has given us and the founders of
other religions and what has been given to their followers
for these reasons: First, that we might see more clearly just
who Jesus Christ is. As one philosopher has said, the only
way that we really understand anything is by knowing
what that thing is. I think we will know more clearly what
Christ is when we look at the rest of the religions of the
world.

Second, let us realize more appreciatively that which we
have been given in Christ, if we are Christians. The fact
that you are a member of a Christian church does not
necessarily mean you are a Christian; but if you are truly a
Christian then I hope that you will see more clearly the
tremendous privilege and blessing you have received.

Third, that we might better understand what our attitude
toward the adherents of non-Christian religions should be.
Should it be one of arrogance or hostility? Hardly! It should
rather be one of pity and compassion and love. Most
Americans do not realize the plight of pagans. They have
visualized some sort of an imaginary person who really
does not represent the great masses of the world that strug-
gle in the dark morass of their paganism. The evolutionist
would tell us that religions are evolved from a polytheistic
animism all the way up to the monotheistic faith of the day,
but the Bible tells us something different. Interestingly
enough, archeologists, in the last fifty years, have been
uncovering one fact after another to show us that, behind
all the vastness of the polytheistic and animistic religions of
the world, there is a basic core and original monotheism
which has been covered up. The Bible tells us that men
originally knew God, but they became vain in their imagi-
nations. Their foolish hearts were darkened and, supposing themselves to be wise, they became fools and worshiped and served the creature rather than the Creator who
is blessed forever. So we find, everywhere, men worship-
ing snakes and creeping things and birds and all sorts of
idols, so that the evolution of religion is in fact a devolution
from the original revelation of God.

The first religion we might consider is one that is held by
hundreds of millions of people around the world from
Africa to the South Seas. It is known as Animism. This is

the religion of the aborigines of most of the continents of the world. It is the primitive people's religion; the most primitive religion on the face of the earth. *Animism* comes from the Latin word which means mind or soul. It is based on the idea that inanimate objects are possessed of a living soul—a living spirit—something which lives within them. Now, they have at least come to discern between the material and the spiritual world. They have a very real consciousness of a spiritual world, and they also have a consciousness of a God who is a single, supreme Being. Every animistic religion of Africa has a word for God . . . but the people are not interested in God, because they believe that He has turned them over to some lesser deities after creating them. They are constantly involved in placating these lesser deities or spirits who are mostly hostile. They also believe that the spirits of people pass into something else—perhaps into a stone or a tree or a crocodile or a river or a bird. It is important to understand animism because it is a substratum that underlies and penetrates every pagan religion. It has elements that can be found in almost every one of them. Here you see the beginning of a concept of the transmigration of the soul or reincarnation that is held in a number of religions. Since these people live in a world which is controlled by savagery and oppression and which has no real moral law, savagery prevails. Animism is a way of darkness. These people live in constant dread and fear of this spiritual world that haunts them everywhere. You often see reverence, dread and awe and worship of such things as snakes found among the animists. Fetishism, black magic, and voodooism are all a part of this horrible primitive religion of man. This is not something for which we would exchange the glories of Christ!

Now, let us go from that to the religions of the great continent of Asia, the subcontinent of Asia—India, and the Hindu religion. Hindu comes from the word *Hind* (from which we get India), and it is indeed the religion of India and was never meant to be evangelistic. To be a Hindu, one must be born one. It originated in about 1500 B.C. at the time when the Israelites were suffering persecution in Egypt. The Aryans, a people from the Iranian plateau and related to the Persians, came into the north of India and conquered the aborigines who were called Dravidians and subjugated these dark-skinned people. This was the beginning of the most basic element of the Hindu religion, "caste." Hinduism is the only religion in the world that has a caste system as part of it. People were divided into castes. Now the Sanskrit word for caste, *varna*, means color. It is a color system of segregation. There are the Brahmans, the highest caste; the Kshatriyas, who are the noblemen; the Vaisyas, who are the mercantile people; and finally the Sudras who are the lowest caste individuals. These people have nothing to do with each other. Furthermore, the low caste has no hope of salvation and cannot even read the sacred books of the Hindus because they are not allowed to come close to a Brahman. A Sudra may come no closer than sixty-four feet to a high caste Brahman lest the air he exhales should contaminate the Brahman. This system developed from a rather simplistic polytheism, where some three hundred and thirty million gods and goddesses were worshiped, to a more sophisticated philosophic pantheism.

In the later writings called the Upanishads, it is presented as Pantheism where everything is God. All is God. There is, according to the teaching of Hinduism, the World Soul, Brahman. This is God and there is a part of this in every one of us. These people feel that the great thing to be understood is that only the World Soul or *atman* is real, and that part of it dwells within us. The rest of the world is an illusion. It does not exist. Our body does not exist. Pain does not exist. Death does not exist. The world does not exist. "All is Brahman and Brahman is all." These people hope through understanding that the world does not really exist and that all is God and that by meditating upon the great existing God, they can finally, through a number of reincarnations, achieve *nirvana*. They feel that this may take thousands of reincarnations of continual suffering. Though the original religion of India was very optimistic, as it progressed it became very pessimistic, which is always true where there is paganism and idolatry. Life becomes worse and worse until these people come to the place where they hate life itself. The great thing they are looking for is the extinction of life. This is *nirvana* where one finally becomes extinct, and ceases to be reborn into further cycles of life; where the individual soul drops back into the ocean and ceases to have any individual consciousness.

About 560 B.C. a Prince of the Sakyas, named Siddhartha Gautama, was born in Northern India. He was wealthy. His father was a Prince and he was kept within a palace and was shielded from all of the world until he was twenty-nine years old. He knew nothing about the suffering of the world. Finally he went out and saw a man who was sick, another who was dying, another who was crippled, and one who was dead. He was so shaken by this experience that he set about to find an answer to the cause of suffering. After six years of searching, he had not found the answer so he finally determined to sit down under a Bo tree and not to get up until he found it. After many days, he finally received enlightenment and discovered the cause of suffering in the world. The Hindu had said the reason for suffering is ignorance. People think that the world is real and therefore they suffer and we must change their thinking. "Not so," says the Buddha, now The Enlightened One. (*Buddha* is related to the word, bode or forebode—to know.) He said the reason is not in the mind nor the intellect. The reason is in the emotions. Buddha was not really a religious founder; he was a psychologist and was concerned about people's emotions—basically about the matter of desire. He said the reason people suffer is that they desire things they cannot have, and, if they would just cease to desire things, they would not suffer any more. If we can just bring our minds to the place where we will cease from all desire then we would cease to suffer. Of course, while Hinduism and Buddhism were both looking for the answer to the problem of suffering, they were looking for the answer to the wrong problem. The problem is sin which did not concern them but which causes suffering. All Buddha had to offer people was simply a quicker way to reach extinction, and, by simply one life, one could leap immediately into the ocean of extinction called *nirvana*. Buddhism is not a religion. Let me quote from a very prestigious Buddhist magazine entitled, *The Buddhist*. It says, "It is etiologically incorrect to refer to Buddhism as a religion." A Buddhist does not admit the existence of God. Buddha was an atheist. He denied any God or gods. He denied prayer. He denied all the priests and the Brahmans. He was a psychologist, as Freud was, and not a religious leader. Buddhism is *not* a religion.

A man by the name of K'ung Fu-tzu, whom we know as Confucius, was born in China in the year 551 B.C. He was a wise man who taught many good things, but he, like Buddha, did not found a religion. He taught filial piety; the relation of subjects to emperors, husbands to wives, par-

ents to children, and elders to youngsters. This is what
Confucius taught. Toward God, he was an agnostic. When
someone asked him, "What about life after death?" He
said, "How can we know about death, when we do not
even know about life?" This is the hope that Confucius
offered—nothing!

Then, of course, there was Shintoism, wherein the emperors of Japan were worshiped. That was given the death
blow in 1945. When you go to Africa you have Islam. There
Mohammed, six hundred years after Christ, gave to the
people the Koran, which is a distortion of much of the Old
Testament of the Bible. It offers a sensual paradise and is a
belief that was spread with the sword. Whereas millions of
Christians died because they were unwilling to renounce
their Christian faith, the Moslems had a strange way of
proselytizing. They took a sword and, if the person was not
willing to become a Moslem, off went his head! They
spread their religion throughout much of North Africa and
Northern India, by conquest, just that way.

Judaism is simply the Biblical religion with its head cut
off—truncated without Christ; the heart of which is a sacrificial system which says that without the shedding of blood
there is no remission of sins. All of the sacrificial system
was ended with the destruction of Jerusalem so now
Judaism has a vacuum at its core. There is nothing else that
men can turn to except Christ. How vastly different are all
these religions from Jesus Christ! There is only one thing
they really have in common. They all teach something
about ethics or about God—not necessarily about both.
Jesus is not just a teacher, as so many people superficially
suppose today. That is not really why He came.

There are three great differences that I would point out to
you between Christ and any other founder of any religion.
They are symbolized by the three great festivals we have in
Christianity. The first is Christmas. Jesus Christ is an incarnate Deity. He is God Himself having come into this
world. Buddha never thought about this. There was no God
anywhere to come to his world. Confucius would have
abhorred the idea. Mohammed would have screamed blasphemy if anyone had suggested that he was God. None of
these people made this claim, but Jesus Christ does. He
claims to be God Almighty before whom every knee shall
bow. His deity is confirmed by a life that is absolutely

unique. His life is unlike any other life that has ever existed. The only sinless life the world has ever known.

Dr. Saunders presents some aspects of the uniqueness of Jesus Christ. I think they are interesting. Let me share them with you. One way in which the life of Jesus Christ was different from anyone that ever existed before or since is: Christ never withdrew or modified any statement He ever made. I wonder how many of you could say the same. How many times I have had to correct my opinion as time has gone on. Jesus never did—not once.

Another thing that we notice about Him is this—He lacked a trait which we have often said is the trait of a great man, and that is the ability, the strength to apologize. When two people have been at odds with each other, I have always said, "You know, I can tell which of you is the larger person—he is the one who apologizes." But Jesus never once apologized for anything He ever did or said. It was not because people never got mad at Him. No matter what the circumstances were, He never apologized. Why? He was never wrong. He, unlike ourselves, was *never* wrong about anything!

Another amazing fact is that He never sought advice from anyone. Though He was born in obscurity, He never sought advice. Unlike Confucius, He was not well educated. He was not educated at all. This Man never learned. He was never taught. Unlike Buddha, He was never enlightened. He always *knew*. Unlike Mohammed, who could neither read nor write, He was never ignorant. He knew everything. He never sought the advice of any soul, though He came to bring a plan to change the world. He went among the doctors and He taught them; He corrected the scribes and the Pharisees. Moses sought seventy advisors and Solomon, the wisest man that ever lived, sought the advice of others, but Jesus never did. He never went to the first grade but He never asked anyone anything. Why? Because He *knew* everything—because He is God.

Another amazing thing is that He never once troubled to justify His ambiguous behavior. When He was asleep in the back of the boat and the storm came and the disciples were rowing and bailing, what was Jesus doing? He was sleeping in the back of the boat! When they roused Him and asked, "Master, carest thou not if we perish?" did He help bail the water out of the boat? No! "O, ye of little

Mark 4:38

Mark 4:39

faith . . . Peace, be still." When Jesus received word that Lazarus had died, He stayed right where He was for four days . . . . Then, when He arrived, Martha said, "Lord,

John 11:21

if Thou hadst been here, my brother would not have died." Did Jesus apologize? No, not a word! He just allowed time and the unfolding of God's plan to justify all that He did.

Another amazing facet of the personality of Jesus is that He never asked for prayer for Himself. How many times have I asked people to pray for me. Jesus never asked anyone to pray for Him. Never! He never even permitted it. What about the three that went into the Garden of Geth-

Mark 13:38

semane? He said, "Come and watch with me." He said, "Pray for *yourselves*, lest *ye* enter into temptation." He never asked anyone to pray for Him. We do not need to pray for God. He never allowed anyone to, and this is amazing because here He was the lowliest of men, the most humble of men that ever lived; and yet He allowed people to fall on their faces before Him and to worship Him. When John did this before an angel, the angel said, "Stand up on

Revelation 22:8

thy feet." But, Jesus never did.

What were Jesus' strong points? He did not have any —not a one! To have a strong point, you must have a weak point and Jesus did not have any weak points. Other men are noted for some one faculty or talent. Moses was the meekest of all men. Job was the patient one, but Jesus was altogether lovely in every way—the meekest, most humble, most patient, most loving, most gracious, most courageous, firmest, wisest, everything—the incomparable symmetry of the perfections of Jesus Christ. What a balance He had! It has been said, "We try so hard to walk that balanced line and we fail so continuously. We try to be spiritual and we end up aesthetic; we try to be liberal in our views of this world and its pleasures and we end up buried under the world; we try to be scrupulous in our conduct and we end up as legalists; we try to follow the high and noble aspirations of liberty and we end up in licentiousness; we try to be fervent and we end up fanatical; we try to be gentle and we waver and fail to follow the truth. But, Jesus mixed truth with gentleness in a perfect mixture. He never once rectified or adjusted His personality because Jesus was God."

Another astounding fact about Him is that He came to do something that the founder of no other religion ever did.

He came to die—not simply to teach—He came to die for our sins. This Confucius did not do. When he was eighty years old, disillusioned by the fact that men would not follow his teachings, he said, "The mountains crumble and the great beam is broken and the flower falls to the ground," and he lay down and died. Buddha died of food poisoning, but Jesus gave His life for the world. What a difference!

Someone said it is like the man in a pit—in a deep, vile, filthy pit with a huge serpent in there with him, that he is trying to avoid. He has fallen into this ghastly pit! What happens? Well, along comes an Animist and he looks down into the pit and sees the serpent. His eyes open wide and he flees into the jungle lest the same evil spirit should heave him into the pit. Then, along comes the Confucianist and he says, "Ah, so, great man never fall in pit, but walk circumspectly and henceforth you will look where you walk." The Hindu comes along and says, "Ah, my brother, you think that you are in a great black pit, but that is the error of mortal mind. The fact is that all is Brahman and Brahman is all and this external world is merely illusion. The pit does not exist. Think, 'There is no pit, there is no pit, there is no serpent, and all will be well . . . peace.' " Then comes the Moslem who sees the man down in the pit and says, "I will help you, my friend," and he reaches down and grabs him by the arm and pulls him halfway out of the pit and draws his knife and says, "however, you will become a Moslem, won't you?" "I can never do that!" So, back he goes into the pit. Then comes the Buddhist who looks down and says, "Dear friend, you are suffering greatly in that pit and the reason you are suffering is because you want to get out of the pit. It is your desire that is making you miserable. What you must come to is a cessation of all desire and then you won't mind being in the pit." And then Jesus comes and looks with compassionate eyes at the man in the pit and into that foul and filthy pit He leaps between the man and the serpent, who rears his ugly head and strikes at the Saviour and sinks his fangs into His side. As the venom of that serpent flows into the blood of Jesus, He lifts the man out of the pit. That, my friends, is a Saviour. That is the difference between Christianity and all the other religions.

Lastly, there is Easter and the Resurrection. Confucius

died and was buried. Lao-tse wandered off and died with his buffalo. Buddha rotted with food poisoning. Jesus rose from the dead and by the Resurrection from the dead He demonstrated that He was indeed the Son of God with power. By His life, by His death, by His Resurrection He declares indeed that He is God Himself.

Napoleon, in his last days, turned to the Scriptures to find the meaning of life, which he had not found in all of his fame, and discovered who Jesus was. He said to General Bertrand, who was an atheist, "I know men; and I tell you that Jesus Christ is not a man. Superficial minds see a resemblance between Christ and the founders of empires, and the gods of other religions. That resemblance does not exist. We can say to the authors of every other religion, 'You are neither gods, nor the agents of the Deity.' What do these gods, so boastful, know more than other mortals; these legislators, Greek or Roman; this Numa; this Lycurgus; these priests of India or of Memphis; this Confucius; this Mohammed?—absolutely nothing. They have made a perfect chaos of mortals. There is not one among them all who has said any thing new in reference to our future destiny, to the soul, to the essence of God, to the creation. Enter the sanctuaries of paganism: you there find perfect chaos, a thousand contradictions, war between the gods, the immobility of sculpture, the division and the rending of unity, the parceling out of the divine attributes mutilated or denied in their essence. It is not so with Christ. Every thing in Him astonishes me. His spirit overawes me, and His will confounds me. Between Him and whoever else in the world, there is no possible term of comparison. He is truly a Being by Himself. Bertrand, if you do not perceive that Jesus Christ is God, very well: then I did wrong to make you a general."

Philippians 2:9

Jesus rose from the dead by the power of the Father who has given Him a name which is above every other name. At the name of Jesus every knee shall bow. Is He the Lord of your life? Is He the Saviour of your life? Friend, have you been so busy with your headlong rush through this hedonism of materialistic America that you have failed even to look around and to consider? Some of you are so blind that you do not even know you are in the pit!

Oh, God, grant us a compassion and pity on those that live in darkness and fear without hope in this life and in the life to come.

We pray that Thou wilt grant us a new zeal to take the love of Jesus Christ and that hope of everlasting bliss which He alone can give to all of the world. And now we pray for any who have never met Him. May they come to know Him personally as they invite Him into their hearts and lives, for we ask it in that blessed name which is above every name even Jesus Christ the Lord. *Amen.*

6 REPENTANCE

I tell you, Nay: but, except ye repent, ye shall all likewise perish.

Luke 13:3

"I tell you, Nay: but, except ye repent, ye shall all likewise perish." These are the words of Jesus Christ concerning repentance. In a way, it's a strange doctrine because repentance itself will not save you. Yet you cannot be saved without it! Merely repenting of one's sin does not guarantee an entrance into heaven. Humanists say all a person must do to enter the Kingdom of Heaven is feel a true contrition for his sins, confess, and repent of them, and endeavor to lead a good life. This is repentance, but not the kind that will gain the forgiveness of our sins or admission into eternal life. Why? Because a person must give Jesus Christ a proper place in his life. You see, God's law has been broken and the transgression of the law demands a penalty must be paid. A change of heart will not suffice.

While many churches ignore this doctrine, the Bible gives it considerable emphasis. Both Old and New Testaments call upon men to repent. Noah was a preacher of righteousness, calling men to leave their wicked ways and turn unto God. All the prophets were preachers of repentance. In fact, *Nahum*'s name comes from a root meaning repentance. Both the major and minor prophets called peo-

Luke 13:3

ple to repent. John the Baptist said: "Repent . . . who hath warned you to flee from the wrath to come? Bring forth therefore fruits meet for repentance."

Matthew 3:7, 8

When Christ reached His thirtieth year (the time for the priest to begin his priestly function), our Great High Priest was baptized and began His work as prophet and priest. How did Jesus begin His ministry? Matthew says: "From that time Jesus began to preach, and to say, Repent . . . ." The burden of His heart and ministry for this world of sinners was: Repent! ". . . Except ye repent, ye shall all likewise perish." Many of His parables, such as the prodigal son, dealt with the subject of repentance. After Jesus' Resurrection, on the road to Emmaus, He said to the two: ". . . Thus it is written, and thus it behoved Christ to suffer, and to rise from the dead the third day: And that repentance and remission of sins should be preached in his name among all nations, beginning at Jerusalem." Christ began, continued, and ended His ministry with the same word—*repent!*

Matthew 4:17

Luke 13:3

Luke 24:46, 47

Acts 2:38

At Pentecost, when the Spirit of God was poured out and the church began its distinctively Christian ministry, Peter preached the first sermon. After the people were reminded what God had done, they said: "What must we do?" And Peter said: "Repent!"

Paul said he was called by God to preach that men should exercise repentance toward God and faith in the Lord Jesus Christ. "And the times of this ignorance God winked at; but now commandeth all men every where to repent." The letters to the churches in the Book of Revelation abound in commands to repent. Eight times in these letters Jesus walks among His churches, symbolic of the churches of all times, and says: ". . . repent . . . or else I will come unto thee quickly, and will remove thy candlestick out of his place." Fifty-three times in the New Testament men are called to repent or told they must have repentance.

Acts 17:30

Revelation 2:5

There are many who delude themselves with the false hope of being in favor with God because of something they may have done. The Westminster Confession says that such hope shall perish with them. Jesus Christ said: ". . . Except ye repent, ye shall all likewise perish." If this is such an essential doctrine, why is it not heralded more clearly from our pulpits today? R. B. Kuiper says that it is because men have lost sight of two things. First, the real meaning of sin; they see it as a trifle, a peccadillo, some-

Luke 13:3

thing they excuse as being part of their human nature. They forget their nature is fallen, debased, depraved, and man is nothing like God first made him. They do not see that sin inevitably brings forth death. And more than this, the root reason is because men have lost their vision of the holy God. They do not lift up their eyes, because if they once saw God, they would abhor themselves and repent in dust and ashes.

Repentance and faith are inseparable in Scripture. There can be no genuine repentance without faith. And there is no genuine faith without repentance. The two go together as heads and tails on one coin. You may have a false faith which is merely an intellectual assent and which brings forth no true repentance or amendment of your life-style; or a repentance without saving faith which causes you to rely upon your own strivings. This becomes a bootstrap repentance where the person endeavors to do better but trusts in his own works.

Because the human soul is made up of mind, heart, and will, all three must become involved in true faith and repentance. We must intellectually grasp that sin, because of its heinousness, will inevitably be punished by God. We must also intellectually grasp and understand the divine remedy for sin. We must come to know the way of salvation as it has been divinely appointed by God and must not be deluded by some false plan of salvation of our own making. We must understand it is only through Christ, His grace, and death on the cross that we have eternal hope. But even understanding will not be sufficient. It must go beyond the mind to the heart, to the affection. We must come to God with a contrite heart. ". . . A broken and contrite heart, O God, thou wilt not despise."

Psalms 51:17

A person may be moved to tears by a sermon and even decide he's going to do something about his sin. But if his decision is not based on a proper understanding of the gospel, he will trust in his own efforts to do better and soon be back wallowing in the mud of sin, despair, and frustration.

There are others who have been reared in the church and suppose themselves to be Christian but have never by an act of their will renounced their sins and turned to Jesus Christ. But nothing less will suffice for repentance! It is only as we see the awfulness of our own sin and truly desire in our hearts to turn from them and embrace the Saviour, that

2 Timothy 2:24, 25

God accepts our repentance. Because this repentance is not something we can do of ourselves; it is not merely an effort to turn over a new leaf and try to do better. 2 Timothy 2:24,25 says: "And the servant of the Lord must not strive; but be gentle . . . instructing those that oppose themselves; if God peradventure will give them repentance . . . ." They glorified God because He granted unto the Gentiles repentance. Repentance then is a gift of God's grace that transforms the heart, mind, and will.

I once heard Jerome Hines sing that memorable part from the *Messiah* which says: "Who shall stand when He appeareth?" My question is: Will you stand in that day? You will not unless you have both repented of your sins and turned to trust in the cross of Christ. You will not unless you have seen your righteousness as nothing but filthy rags; unless you have seen all of your good deeds as tainted with self, vanity, and pride. You will not unless you have trusted only in the righteousness of Christ and His atoning blood.

Revelation 20:12–15

Have you repented of your sins or are you deluded into believing that you can live in sin and then live in heaven? The Word of Christ to you is unmistakable. In that great day they shall come forth from the graves—the rich and poor, wise and foolish, righteous and unrighteous, wicked and saints, rulers and slaves, great men and small. From the depth of the sea, the ships shall give up their dead; those that have lain long in cemeteries shall come forth. When Christ shall speak, they shall hear His voice and all come forth—willing and unwilling. They shall arise. They shall stand before God. *And they shall be judged.* Only if our names are written in the Lamb's Book of Life will we enter into eternal life. Will your name be written there?

Luke 13:3

Jesus Christ says: "Except ye repent, ye shall all likewise perish."

O God, deliver us from being deceived. Grant unto us a new sense of the heinousness of our sins and the holiness of God. May we turn from them all to walk in the ways of new obedience. Cause us to mourn for our sins and turn unto Thee, O Lord Jesus Christ, who has been lifted up on a cross that we might be saved if we will repent and believe. *Amen.*

7 FAITH

For by grace are ye saved through faith; and that not of your-
selves: it is the gift of God: Not of works, lest any man should
boast.

Ephesians 2:8, 9

The occasion was a typical Sunday church service, but
the locale was behind the iron curtain in Communist East
Europe. The service was progressing as usual when suddenly two Communist soldiers brandishing submachine
guns kicked open the door. With flailing arms and angry
voices, they denounced the Christians and their vile worship. "Such worms as you have no right to exist upon the
face of the earth!" they shouted. "We are going to shoot all
of you! However, those who are willing to denounce their
faith and deny Christ can move immediately to the right
side of the sanctuary and you will be free to leave." A
portion of the congregation got up and moved. The soldiers
then commanded them to get out. Most of the congregation
sat motionless in their pews. When the doors were closed,
the Communists turned to those sitting before them. "We,
too, are Christians," they said. "We've come to fellowship
with you but we first had to get rid of the hypocrites."

I like this story because it perfectly illustrates this important matter of faith. Faith is important because it is the key
that opens the door to the Christian life and all Christ has

Mark 16:16

done for us. It's the key that opens the door to heaven. The Scripture says: "He that believeth . . . shall be saved; but he that believeth not shall be damned."

I would like to consider this matter in three aspects: First, the nature of faith; second, the object of faith; third, the origin of faith. Many people bring themselves to church to hear words they have not the slightest intention of obeying. This is exceedingly strange when we consider the secular world where belief and faith are easily understood.

If, for instance, a person is told his business venture is entirely spurious and is presented with the facts as to why this is so, he will listen to the reasons, and then decide to accept or reject them. If he believes, he immediately removes all property from the misrepresented venture. If someone comes to you and says in desperate tones: "The rear of your house is on fire!" and you believe him, you will immediately leap from your chair, call the fire department, and flee from the premises with your family.

If a man is shown an X ray that contains a dark and ominous spot representing sure death unless he takes immediate steps for its removal, and if he believes the diagnosis, he will immediately place himself in the surgeon's hands. There is no question about it!

Belief in the secular world is plain, simple, and understood by all, but when we come to Christian truth, things seem to change. Most hear over and over again that the "wages of sin is death . . . God is angry with the wicked every day . . . He that believeth not shall be damned . . . [God] will by no means clear the guilty . . . except ye repent, ye shall all likewise perish." Those who are ashamed of Christ here in this world will find He is ashamed of them in the world to come. They hear also that God offers forgiveness, a gracious salvation, eternal life, and this offer will not continue indefinitely. They hear a time is coming when the day of grace will irretrievably be gone and the opportunity lost. They know for them this moment is completely uncertain. They know in a moment they have not considered, there may be a sudden pain in the chest, or a screeching of brakes and crashing of glass, and death will transport them into eternal woe.

This they hear, but, though God calls loudly and clearly to change from one path of life to enter upon another, they neglect to do anything about it. By a calculation of chances,

Romans 6:23
Psalms 7:11
Mark 16:16
Exodus 34:7
Luke 13:13

on which they would not risk so much as a penny in the mercantile world, they deceive and assure themselves that they are able to face such a risk. Though they hear these words often, many do not practice the truths they have heard. Professing to believe, they act throughout the week in point-blank opposition to what they have heard on Sunday. Such is the condition of vast multitudes of people who call themselves Christians.

Now the question I propose is this: Does such indolent assent deserve the name of faith? Do these people in fact believe? Place this question before any secular jury and the verdict would be inevitable. When somebody in the secular world believes in a business deal, they act on it. Regardless of what you might have thought about the people who fled that morning from the church in East Europe, there is one unmistakable thing—they believed the soldiers! The man who tells you he believes what you've told him about his business picture and does nothing about it, only invites you to doubt his word. The man who says: "Oh, the house is on fire? Yes, of course . . ." and then goes back to reading the sports page, is telling you he doesn't believe you. The man, who leaves the doctor's office and does nothing as a result of the declaration of the physician, is simply declaring to the world that he does not believe the diagnosis. The secular world is not befuddled; it knows what *believe* means. It knows that if a person believes something concerning a matter which involves action, they will *inevitably* do that which their belief demands.

The principle is exactly the same in religious matters. He who does not act upon what he has heard is simply a man who does not believe. The man, who is not moved to a correspondent action or volition by what he hears, is a man without faith. Martin Luther said that many people suppose themselves to have faith but they don't know what it is. True faith is a divine work of God in our hearts which makes us new men in all our faculties. It is a busy, active thing which doesn't stop to ask if good works should be done. To put it in the words of our Confession of Faith: We are justified by faith alone. It is faith alone which is the instrument of justification. That faith which alone justifies is never alone in the justified individual. It is always accompanied by those graces which will inevitably be produced by a living faith. James said: ". . . Faith without works is dead," which simply means that a faith which does not produce a transformed life is a vain, empty illusion and is no real faith at all.

There have been many long dissertations on the matter of faith—most of which confuse more than clarify. Innumerable theologians have given themselves sedulously to distinguish the various types of faith, various organs of believing, various types of mental assent, et cetera. The average layman who reads such works comes to the conclusion that faith is something which is reserved for the mystical saint or the obtuse theologian. Though the Bible says, if they

believe, they will have eternal life, they find themselves incapable of understanding what is meant by belief. The faith that justifies is not something different in nature from that which we know as faith and believing.

How did Christ begin His ministry? Did He begin by establishing a school where He spent the first year or so in long theological and philosophical arguments about the nature of this new thing called faith that He was going to reveal to the world? And after many dissertations and explanations about the meaning of faith, did He say to the people: "Now that you know what *believe* means, you can believe." He did no such thing! Rather, we read in Scrip-

ture: "Jesus began to preach and to say, repent and believe." Throughout Scripture there is every indication that Jesus used the word *believe* and *faith* in a way that all would understand. There was nothing confusing about it. Thus, to have faith is to believe; to believe is to have faith.

When I come to see something is true (not merely understanding it, but seeing it is true), then I have faith in it—whether I like it or not. I may accept it willingly or I may accept it unwillingly. But if I believe it to be true, then indeed I have faith in it. This is the meaning of faith.

Perhaps you think you do believe but don't have the temperament or disposition to serve Christ, to give yourself unstintingly for Him, to bear witness to His Gospel as He commands, to read His Scripture, to pray, to fulfil His Great Commission, and indeed endeavor by all you have within you to walk in the ways of complete and new obedience. No, it's not that there is something different about your disposition. What I would have you see is that you do not believe. Coiled deep down in your soul is the lurking serpent of unbelief. If you believed, you would be transformed by that belief. ". . . If any man be in Christ, he is a

new creature [a new creation] . . . ." This is the nature of
belief; there is nothing confusing about it. Do you believe
the Word of God? Our Confession of Faith states it clearly
that by this faith a Christian believeth to be true whatsoever is revealed in the Word, for the authority of God
Himself speaking therein. There it is. He believes it to be
true. When you truly believe something to be true, you will
invariably act according to it. Therefore, the problems with
our behavior are simply evidences of our unbelief.

What are we to believe? What is the object of our faith? In
the broadest sense, it is the whole Word of God; whatsoever is revealed in His Word. And we act differently
upon each particular passage—yielding obedience to the
commands and embracing the promises of God for this life
and that which is to come. It is believing the Word of God.
This is faith. But this is a faith which inevitably works by
love. The supreme object of our faith is the person of Jesus
Christ Himself. As our Confession continues, the principal
acts of saving faith are accepting, receiving, and resting
upon Christ alone for justification, sanctification, and eternal life. This is the principal act of saving faith: Receiving
Him, resting upon Christ who comes to us in all His grace
and glory as our High Priest, our Sacrifice, our Surety, who
offers Himself in our stead, and who promises us eternal
life. Our accepting of Him is based upon the promises of
God's Word. Jesus Christ said: "He that believeth on Me
hath everlasting life . . . ; Him that cometh unto Me I will
in no wise cast out; He that believeth on Me shall not be
condemned." Faith is believing to be true what God has
said.

Many of those who do not have faith are those who
believe some false or distorted notion which does not allow
them to understand or believe what God's Word says. They
suppose the Bible presents Christ as a taskmaster requir-
ing them to do something to save themselves. They do not
understand Jesus Christ is not a taskmaster but indeed our
Surety who fulfilled God's demands and died for our sins.
When we come to believe His Word and trust in Him, we
are reconciled to God, our sins are forgiven, we are made
heirs of eternal life, adopted into His family, and become
the children of God. When we believe that we are saved,
our lives are invariably transformed.

But why the problem of unbelief? The problem is we are
blind and cannot see Him because Satan has deluded our

2 Corinthians 5:17

John 3:16
John 6:37
John 3:18

Mark 8:18

John 3:3

minds. Jesus said: "Ye have eyes and see not." Blind! Groping in darkness! Christ said: "Except a man be born again, he cannot see the kingdom of God"—much less enter into it!

After talking to a lovely young lady about the meaning of Christ, I said, "If you really want Him to come into your heart, go home and ask Him to come in, to open your eyes, and to give you eternal life." She called several days later to tell me she had received Christ. "And," she said, "for the first time in my life the worship service means something to me. It's a whole new world!"

John 3:3

"Except a man be born again, he cannot see the kingdom of God." Faith comes by the Spirit of God at work in our hearts and yet many cannot believe because their hearts are hardened in sin. But I say to you: look unto Him who has died in your place and paid your penalty. Look unto Him whose hands are extended unto you and offering you life eternal. There is life for a look at the Crucified One. Look—and believe!

Father, we pray that Your Spirit may graciously and sovereignly open the eyes of the blind that they may see the light of Your glory shining in the face of Jesus Christ. May they take hold of Him by faith and be transformed by His love. In His lovely Name, *Amen.*

8 JUSTIFICATION

Therefore we conclude that a man is justified by faith without the deeds of the law.

Romans 3:28

In this chapter, we come to the pinnacle of the *ordo salutis*—the way of salvation—we come to holy ground. We come to the great central theme of the doctrines of redemption in the Church of Christ. We come to *justification*. This is that doctrine which broke the shackles from the soul of Martin Luther and set him free, exalting in his God and glorying in the mercy of Jesus Christ. This is that doctrine which he took upon his tongue and with flaming eloquence proclaimed all over Europe. This is that doctrine which became the very heartbeat of the Protestant Reformation. This is that doctrine without which there would be no Protestantism. John Calvin said, "This is the foremost pillar of religion." The great Geerhadus Vos said, "It is the pivotal point around which all else turns." The immortal Bavinck said, "This is the article of the creed by which the Church either stands or falls."

The doctrine of justification *is* the Gospel of our Lord Jesus Christ. Here the full-orbed mercy and grace of God comes into its own. But, alas, we live in a time almost like that of Luther's. The darkness of spiritual ignorance has so pervaded the minds of men that vast numbers of people in this so-called Christian America live in abject ignorance of this central teaching of the Christian faith; this central doctrine of the Bible. I think it can be safely said that without at least a rudimentary knowledge of the basic principle involved in this doctrine, no person will ever see heaven. Truly by this the Church stands or falls and our souls stand or fall with it. If this be the case then, indeed, most of the Church is sadly fallen in our day. And how great is that fall! From that time, only 450 years ago, when this was the clarion call—the trumpet blast—that woke countless hundreds of thousands from their death in sin unto life eternal, we have come to our time when in myriads of churches across our land the question "What is justification?" would meet merely with a raised eyebrow and a questioning look. *"The just shall live by faith"* was the watchword of the Protestant Reformation.

Let us now consider the nature of this doctrine and its importance to us. In this doctrine lies the truth that answers the greatest need that man has: How can man be rightly related to God? In the Book of Job, probably the oldest book of the Bible, Job cries out from the depths of his heart, asking how a sinful man can ever stand in the presence of a Holy God. This is the cry that has been wrung from the blanched lips of countless millions of penitent sinners down through the centuries. But it is a cry that is strangely unheard in our day. Why? Well, the reason is not hard to come by. I think it is very simply that man is so abysmally far from God for the most part that he is even ignorant of the fact he is separated from God. He has no concept whatsoever of sin. He has no feeling of remorse for it. He has no awareness of the righteousness and holiness of God and, consequently, no feeling of any need for justification. He can quite adequately justify himself in his own eyes. If sin is considered at all, it is merely a peccadillo of some sort to be easily rationalized away, or at most adjusted by a visit to the psychiatrist.

John Murray, the famous theologian, has presented our predicament very tersely in these words: "How can man be right with God? The answer, of course, is that we cannot be right with Him for we are all wrong with Him. And we are all wrong with Him because we have all sinned and come short of the glory of God. Far too frequently we fail to entertain the gravity of this fact; hence the reality of our sin and the reality of the wrath of God upon us for our sin do

Book of Job

not come into our reckoning at all. This is the reason why the grand article of justification does not ring the bells in the innermost depths of our souls today. And this is the reason why the gospel of justification is to such an extent a meaningless sound in the world of the church of the twentieth century. We are not imbued with the profound sense of the reality of God; of His majesty and His holiness. And sin, if reckoned with at all, is little more than a misfortune or a maladjustment. If we are to appreciate that which is central in the gospel, if the jubilee trumpet is to find its echo again in our hearts, our thinking must be revolutionized by the realism of the wrath of God, of the reality and gravity of our guilt, and of the divine condemnation upon it."

Those are words that are seldom heard in our day when sin is glossed over, ignored, or snickered at—but God is not impressed with our light attitude toward that which He hates. God has sworn that He will "visit [our] transgression with the rod, and [our] iniquity with stripes." There is a divine penalty for sin. Twentieth century man has endeavored to forget it, to deny it, to ignore it, to turn his back upon it, to get away from it, to escape from it, and hope in some way that it will just go away and leave him alone. But it will not! The reality of man's guilt has filled to overflowing the mental institutions of this nation until they sprawl as endless cities. Wing after wing of these institutions is filled with people who are there primarily because their lives are overwhelmed and crushed by their guilt which they've striven to ignore and to deny.

Psalms 89:32

When will we face reality for the way it is and seek God's remedy for it instead of our own daubing at the surface blemishes of the fatal cancer within? Even Freud, unbeliever that he was, in his psychoanalytic studies probed deep into the soul of men. There, as he plunged down into that subbasement of the human soul which he called the id, he found lurking in all of the crevices and corners of that soul such foulness, such unbelievable hate, such attitudes towards those whom they were supposed to love, such lust and greed and pride, that he himself was shocked at what he discovered. But he was unknowingly putting his imprimatur on the Word of God which says, "For all have sinned, and come short of the glory of God . . . . The heart is deceitful . . . and desperately wicked: who can know it? I the Lord search the heart . . . ."

Romans 3:23

Jeremiah 17:9, 10

It is not until the Apostle Paul has impressed upon us this fact of our guilt that he even begins to bring up the subject of justification. In the first chapter of the Book of Romans, his theme is: All the Gentiles have sinned and God has given them up to condemnation. In the second chapter his theme is: All of the Jews have sinned and God has given them up to condemnation. In the third chapter his theme is: All, both Jews and Gentiles, are under sin; there is no difference—"For all have sinned and come short of the glory of God . . . . Therefore by the deeds of the law there shall no flesh be justified in his sight. . . ." It is only at that point, when every man and woman on the face of this planet is shut up under sin, that Paul brings in the new revelation of the mercy of God: "But now the righteousness of God is revealed." It is a free righteousness coming from God: "Being justified freely by his grace . . . ."

Romans 3:23

Romans 3:20

Romans 3:21

Romans 3:24

What then is the nature of this justification? The Westminster Catechism describes it most beautifully and aptly when it says that justification is an act of God's free grace wherein He pardoneth all our sins and accepteth our persons as righteous—not for anything done by us or wrought in us, but only for the righteousness of Jesus Christ imputed to us and received by faith alone. Let us see what that means. First of all, we see that *it is an act of God.* It is God that justifieth. Who is he who condemneth? Man is constantly trying to justify himself. Someone said to me one time, "I can justify everything I've ever done to God." And though few people would be so rash as to make such a statement, this is exactly what most people are trying to do. I hear it constantly. They're trying to justify themselves; they're trying to plead innocent. "I'm not really so bad. I've really done some good. I've done this . . . I haven't done those most wicked things . . . ." They're trying to justify themselves.

The doctrine of justification condemns every effort on the part of man to justify himself. It is God that justifieth—not man. It is an act—not a process. It is done in the twinkling of the eye. In an instant, it is complete and perfect forever. It is an act of God's own free grace. We see that it flows from the graciousness of Almighty God. It is not because of anything that we have done. We are not justified for our works; we are not justified because of our character; we are not justified because of our virtue or our goodness, of which the natural man in his unregenerate state has not one whit. We are justified purely by the grace and unmerited favor of God.

It is not anything done by us or *wrought in us*. Justification does not change our hearts, our souls, our lives one whit. It is something which is external to us. It is something which is declared about us by God. It is not God acting as a doctor or a surgeon in which He comes in and changes our hearts. Indeed God does internally change us, but that is regeneration and sanctification. Justification—that act whereby we begin the Christian life—is something which is outside of us altogether. It is a declaration about us; the declarative act of a Judge about a sinner. In this declaration, God declares us to be righteous.

Some people have difficulty here. First of all, they do not understand what the word *justify* means. Let me say that it does not mean to make holy; it does not mean to make virtuous; it does not mean that it makes you good. You are no better the moment after you are justified than you were the moment before. You are not one bit holier the moment after you are justified than you were before. We cannot separate justification and sanctification. God has placed His Spirit within us and He is going to continue to work to sanctify us. But our justification is not something that comes at the end of this process when we have reached a certain level of acceptableness. We are justified as ungodly sinners. God justifies the ungodly. How could He do this? Justify does not mean to make holy.

But God justifieth the *ungodly*. That this is true is evidently supported by the scriptural use of the word *to justify*. It is everywhere used as the opposite and antithesis of the word *to condemn*. The Bible says that just judges are to justify the righteous and condemn the wicked. The Bible says it is an abomination in the sight of God if a judge justifies the wicked and condemns the righteous. It is a declaration about a person—not a change of his internal nature.

For example, "All the people . . . and the publicans, justified God," the Bible says. It would be absurd to suppose that a sinful publican could make God holy. They merely declared what He was. The Bible says that it is a sin for a man to declare someone that is wicked to be righteous. But that's exactly what God does. And yet He does it without sin. How is it that He can do it? He does it in that wonderful way which is the gospel. He does it through His

Son the Lord Jesus Christ. We are justified freely by His grace through the redemption that is in Christ Jesus, whom God hath set forth as a propitiation—a sacrifice—for our sins in order that He might be both the just and the justifier of him that believeth in Jesus. It is through Christ that God does this.

The work of Christ may be divided into two parts. Theologians describe it as the *active* and the *passive* obedience of Christ. First of all, there are the thirty-three years in which He lived a perfect life, totally obeying every command of God. What kind of life does God require of you if you would ever enter heaven? He requires a perfect life. Do you have it? "Be ye therefore perfect, even as your Father which is in heaven is perfect." No, you don't have it. But Christ lived it for you—perfectly, vicariously, in your stead—and that life He is willing to give to you. The passive obedience of Christ (from which we get the word *passion*) is that which Christ endured for us, that which He suffered for us, primarily upon the cross. It is on the cross that Christ takes away all of our sin, all of our debt. But it is by His life, His active obedience, that we are given a perfect righteousness whereby we can stand in the presence of God.

Matthew 5:48

If, as some suppose, justification were to be identified merely with forgiveness of sins, then we would merely be forgiven and brought to the place that Adam started. We would still have to work out our own righteousness which Adam with his perfect nature was unable to do. (How much less would we be able to do it!) Therefore, in the act of justification God does two things. He first constitutes us righteous by imputing to our account the perfect righteousness of Jesus Christ. Having done this, He thereby declares what the situation then is. He thereby declares that the demands of the law have been met in our case, as Christ has fulfilled all of the obligations that we have to the law of God. He first *constitutes* us righteous and then *declares* us so to be; but it is with the righteousness of His Son. It might be somewhat analogous to graciously giving a man a large sum of money and then declaring him to be wealthy. This is what God does. He grants unto us the perfect righteousness of His Son and then declares us to be righteous. The Bible says that through the disobedience of one man, many were accounted or constituted as sinners, so also through the obedience of One many were constituted righteous through the righteousness of Jesus Christ.

see Genesis 3

The doctrine of justification is infinitely more than mere forgiveness. A governor or executive may forgive a criminal; a judge may pardon one; and yet no judge has ever yet constituted a pardoned criminal righteous. Nor has he ever adopted him into his family; nor has he ever given him an inheritance; nor has he ever given unto him his name. But all of these things and many others God has done for us. He declares us to be righteous only through the righteousness of Jesus Christ our Lord.

We must all some day stand before God. With what righteousness will you approach that awful throne? In that great day, when the heavens shall melt with fervent heat, and the earth shall be burnt up, and all of the elements, how will you approach unto the throne of God? Isaiah the prophet describes it for us in this way: "I will greatly rejoice in the Lord, my soul shall be joyful in my God; for he hath clothed me with the garments of salvation, he hath covered me with the robe of righteousness, as a bridegroom decketh himself with ornaments, and as a bride adorneth herself with her jewels." As the hymn says,

Isaiah 61:10

> Jesus, Thy blood and righteousness,
> My beauty are, my glorious dress;
> Midst flaming worlds, in these arrayed,
> With joy shall I lift up my head.

This is the nature of justification. How do we receive it? We receive it by faith; simply trusting in Christ. "Nothing in my hand I bring, simply to thy cross I cling." But there's a problem here for many. You see, this is such a humbling thing. It requires that we, like the Apostle Paul, look at all of those so-called "good works" we have done that once were our pride and joy and now count as dung, that we may be found in Christ. We have not our own righteousness, which comes from trying to keep the law and in which we fail miserably every day, but we have the righteousness of God which is by faith in Jesus Christ. It's a humbling thing. We have to admit our spiritual and moral bankruptcy, and this is what goes against the grain of the proud man and smites him right in the forehead.

The brilliant Dr. Gerstner has described the plight of the proud man in this way: "Christ has done everything necessary for his salvation. Nothing now stands between the sinner and God but the sinner's 'good works.' Nothing can keep him from Christ but his delusion that he does not need Him—that he has good works of his own that can satisfy God. If men will only be convinced that they have no righteousness that is not as filthy rags; if men will see that there is none that doeth good, no, not one; if men will see that all are shut up under sin—then there will be nothing to prevent their everlasting salvation. All they need is need. All they must have is nothing. All that is required is acknowledged guilt. But, alas, sinners cannot part with their 'virtues.' They have none that are not imaginary, but they are real to them. So grace becomes unreal. The real grace of God they spurn in order to hold on to the illusory virtues of their own. Their eyes fixed on a mirage, they will not drink real water. They die of thirst in the midst of an ocean of Grace."

So, my friend, to what do you cling? Is it the illusory mirage of your own righteousness? Would you hug your fig leaves around you to cover the nakedness of your soul? Or will you come to Christ to be cleansed by His blood and clothed with His righteousness, that He might present you faultless before His throne with exceeding joy?

There will be one day, says Christ, a great wedding feast. And all that come there will have on the beautiful white wedding garments—a picture of the righteousness of Christ. In the parable in Matthew, there came a man that had not on a wedding garment. And the king came out to look at his guests. His eyes fixed upon the one man there that had not on a wedding garment and he said unto him, "Friend, how camest thou hither? How dare you come into this presence dressed in such vile and foul rags?" Ah, but he had supposed that he was dressed in his Sunday best —all of his Sunday-school deeds, his character, his morality, his money given to charity, his commandment keeping, his Golden-Rule living—he thought that he was just the nicest dressed person there! Then the lights went on and he saw himself for what he was—foulness from head to foot! And the command came down to that one who was speechless: "Bind him hand and foot, and take him away, and cast him into outer darkness; there shall be weeping and gnashing of teeth."

To what are you clinging? In what are you trusting? Your righteousness or Christ's? Your merit or His? We are justified freely by His grace through the redemption that is in Christ Jesus.

Margin notes:

Matthew 22:10–12

Matthew 22:13

"Foul, [we] to the fountain fly: Wash [us], Saviour, or [we] die." Lord enlighten our minds by Thy Spirit that we may see ourselves as we really are, despise our sins, trust not in our own righteousness, but flee to the cross. And embracing it may we be cleansed by Thy blood, O Christ, within, and clothed in Thy precious righteousness, without, that thus we may be justified from all of our sins and be fit to enter eternal life. Through Thy blessed name we pray. *Amen.*

9 SANCTIFICATION

Sanctify them through thy truth: thy word is truth. And for their sakes I sanctify myself, that they also might be sanctified through the truth.

John 17:17, 19

"Away with vain words . . . . Christianity is life—not doctrine . . . . Our only creed is Christ . . . . Let us be done with dogma and go on to duty." Familiar words? Do you believe them? Millions have. And with such shibboleths as these, the axe has been laid to the root of genuine Christianity by Satan himself. "For as [a man] thinketh in his heart, so is he." If there is anything peculiar to the Protestant churches which emerges from the Reformation, it is this: All life must be grounded in truth. That which a man believes is going to determine what he does, and the life we live will spring inevitably from the beliefs that we hold. This is why we are saved by faith, and faith is the belief of the truth and the reception of it as such.

Christianity, indeed, is not only life, but it is also doctrine. It is a life which is produced by belief. Those who would castigate creed and dogma and doctrine should perchance take a look again at what these words mean. The word *doctrine* comes from the Latin word *docēre*, which means to teach. The word *creed* comes from the Latin word *credo*, which means I believe. The word *dogma* comes from a

Proverbs 23:7

83

Greek word *dokeō* which means to think. Therefore, a person who has no dogma, no creed, and no doctrine is a person who neither thinks, believes, or teaches. But if you are going to think anything, believe anything, and teach anything, then, my friends, you need dogma, creed, and doctrine. This is the substance which forms the foundation of the Christian faith.

The problem with so many today is that they do have dogma, doctrine, and creed, but they are usually of their own making. They have mixed them up and brewed them in their own minds. The problem is not that they do not hold such, but that which they hold is corrupted by untruth and falsehood. This is the reason for the low state of morality and the apathy which is rampant in this country and the Church today.

If we are going to have a vital life in the Church, then that life must spring from the truth. Abraham Kuyper, the great Dutch theologian, gave this illustration: There was a time in centuries gone by when outside in the world there was only darkness and freezing cold, yet in the Church there was warmth and joy and zeal, as men warmed themselves beside the fires of the truth of the Word of God. But those fires became corrupted with untruth. Slowly they dimmed and went out and a chill settled on the Church. Those inside became aware of their condition and their coldness and they bestirred themselves to do something about it. There arose in their midst those who gave to them an answer for their problem. "You see, gentlemen," they said, "you can get no heat from fires. The thing to do is to remove the fireplace entirely and create the heat in your own soul without the use of fire. Simply rub your hands together hard enough and soon you will be warm." But the Biblical answer is to light again the fires of truth. This is the prayer of Jesus Christ. "Sanctify them through thy truth: thy word is truth."

John 17:17

We have come in our series of doctrinal studies to the doctrine of sanctification. This is an exceedingly important doctrine because it reaches us right where we are. This has to do with our Christian life as we are living it right now. There are many who have said, "Certainly this is such a simple doctrine that it could not be corrupted with falsehood. It is merely living the Christian life, so we need not worry about the doctrine of sanctification; let us have the fact of sanctification." But the problem is that today not one church member in ten has the foggiest notion of what the biblical doctrine of sanctification really is. This is the reason, I believe, there is so little true sanctification in the Church today. Sanctification is a doctrine as well as a life.

What is the biblical doctrine of sanctification? With what does it deal? What is its nature? What is its origin? What are its means? Sanctification is closely related to the doctrine of justification which we studied earlier. Since these are often confused, we need to distinguish them. Though they can never be separated, they must be distinguished. According to the Reformers, the confusion of the doctrine of sanctification and the doctrine of justification was one of the principal errors of the Church of Rome which teaches that, if we become sufficiently sanctified, we shall in the end thereby be justified. But the Bible teaches that we are justified first, and this results in our sanctification.

Let us look at these two terms and see if we can grasp the difference between sanctification and justification. First of all, justification is an act; sanctification is a process. Justification takes place once for all and is complete and perfect; sanctification is imperfect and is a long process which lasts from the beginning of the Christian life until the moment we die. Justification is something which is external to us; sanctification is something which happens within us. Justification, in its metaphorical sense, is the act of a judge (what a judge declares about us); sanctification is more the work of a surgeon (something done within us). Justification is something which is declared about us—that we are not guilty and are declared to be righteous; sanctification is something which is done to us.

Having now grasped these few distinctions between the two doctrines, let us further consider the difference and the purpose of these two works of God. Both of them have to do with two very different aspects of sin, for sin according to the Scriptures has two aspects. If you do not distinguish these in your own mind, you will have great difficulty understanding Christian theology.

The *first aspect of sin* is what is known as guilt. Guilt is "liability to punishment." I would not want you to confuse that with guilt feelings which are played up so strongly in so many of our psychological writings today and strangely enough even by those who deny the reality of guilt. If a person breaks a law in the civil realm, they are now liable to punishment if they are caught. This is guilt. We who sin against the law of God are liable to punishment. The *second aspect of sin* is something within us, and that is "corruption." Thus, the two aspects of sin are guilt and corruption. Guilt is something which is outside of us (not guilt feelings). It has to do with our relationship to the law. Corruption has something to do with what is inside of us—our corrupted natures.

God is going to deal with both of these aspects of sin. He deals with the matter of guilt through justification. It is a judge who deals with guilt. In the act of justification, the righteousness of Christ is imputed to us and we are declared to be righteous as far as our relationship to the law is concerned. This is done once for all. We do not grow in righteousness. We are no more justified twenty years after we have accepted Christ than we were the moment we accepted Him. We are given the perfect righteousness of Christ. We are clothed with the garment of salvation and covered with the robe of righteousness. But sanctification is doing away with our corruption and this is done not by the imputation of the righteousness of Christ to us, once for all, but by the gradual infusion of the holiness of Christ into us. Both our righteousness and our holiness come from Christ.

Let us pause for a moment to see if we understand the difference between these two aspects of sin: guilt and corruption. Instead of guilt, what we need is righteousness in the sight of the law, and instead of corruption, what we need is holiness.

It is here that people have difficulty grasping the matter of holiness. Perhaps you might grasp it better if you thought of it in terms of this illustration. Is there anyone who doesn't know what is meant when they unknowingly bite into an apple and find it to be corrupt? Perhaps the term rotten would be a little more familiar. This is simply to say that in the sight of God all of us are rotten apples. That is corruption.

If that doesn't jolt your sensibilities enough, may I point out to you that there is also another result of rottenness. If you leave a rotten apple around long enough, it will begin to have a strange odor. God says we are a stench in His nostrils. Now that's not very pleasant but that is God's portrait of mankind. From the top of our heads to the soles of our feet, there is nothing but corruption within us. Therefore, we need the holiness of Jesus Christ. In English the word *holiness* comes from the word *whole*—wholeness, soundness, oneness. If anyone were able to make a rotten apple sound, that would be an amazing feat. We know how to make a good apple rotten, but how do we make a rotten apple good? Only God can do this. One of the general reasons that apples rot is that they are taken off the tree. You take any apple off a tree and leave it around long enough and it's going to get rotten. If we are severed from the Vine, we are going to become corrupt and rotten. Holiness is an attribute of God alone and any holiness, which exists in anyone or anything in this world, exists only because it is related to God. The holiness of God has flowed into it in some way. The purpose and object of sanctification is to make us holy in the sight of God.

Having been justified, we are removed from our liability to punishment; we are declared innocent and not guilty. Having been clothed with the garments of Christ, we now need to become holy within. The Bible says that God is of purer eyes than to look upon iniquity . . . that all sin, whether it is in an unbeliever or a believer, is contrary to the holiness of God and is an abomination in His sight. He despises sin. The commandment of God to us is ". . . and ye shall be holy; for I am holy." This is the matter to which sanctification addresses itself. God commands us to become holy. "Without holiness no man shall see God," is the teaching of the Bible. We are to perfect holiness in the fear of the Lord. If there is anything that the Church of Christ needs today, it is a view of the holiness and majesty of God and a consequent view of His demands upon us that we are to be holy as He is holy. Are you holy?

Habakkuk 1:13

Leviticus 11:44

"For all that is in the world, the lust of the flesh, and the lust of the eyes, and the pride of life, is not of the Father, but is of the world. And the world passeth away, and the lust thereof." These are not of the Father. They are vile in His sight; they are rotten. And yet we live in such a rotten world. Those who come to see the glory of God will cry out in their anguish saying, "O God, I am a man of unclean lips and I dwell in the midst of a people with unclean lips. I have seen the Lord of hosts and I abhor myself in dust and ashes."

1 John 2:16

Isaiah 6:5

What is your particular form of corruption? Is it the lust of the flesh? God calls us to holiness in body, mind, and spirit. Anything which is contrary—any rottenness, any corruption—God demands that it be replaced by that

Matthew 5:28

which is sound and holy. How many minds today are virtually pornographic? How about the body, which God commands be presented unto Him as a living sacrifice, holy, and therefore acceptable in His sight? Is your body holy? Or is it contaminated with all manner of vile deeds and habits? Is your spirit holy? What about the lust of the eyes (covetousness)? The Bible says that covetousness is a corruption in His sight. How about the pride of life? Vain ambition . . . seeking to be better than our neighbors . . . keeping up with the Joneses . . . pride in our appearance . . . pride in our knowledge . . . pride in our ability. The pride of life is another form of vile rottenness, says He who can say,

Matthew 11:29

". . . learn of me; for I am meek and lowly in heart."

Without holiness, no man shall see God. Whence then are we to obtain this? Sanctification is not merely an effort on the part of Christians to live a better Christian life. In fact, sanctification is not really the effort of man at all; sanctification is the work of God. It is God that sanctifies. Salvation is of God, whether it be justification in the past tense, or sanctification in the present tense, or glorification in the future when the final vestiges of sin are removed. Salvation is wholly of God. It is God that sanctifies.

The agent of sanctification is not man but the Holy Spirit. It is the infusing of the holiness of Christ. There is no holiness in us. A rotten apple could jump up and down, bestir itself, clap its hands and do whatever it wanted to and it would still be nothing more than a rotten apple. And so there is nothing about ourselves that can make us holy.

This does not mean that we are passive in sanctification. We are passive in regeneration but we are active in our sanctification, though it is still all of grace. We are to make use of the means of sanctification which are the Word of God, prayer, obedience to all of God's commandments, the sacraments, and worship. The Holy Spirit takes our use of these means and makes them the method by which He sanctifies us. But let me remind you that you could read the Word of God until you were green in the face, and you could pray until your knees were worn smooth, and you would not be sanctified one bit if the Holy Spirit of God does not sanctify you. Therefore, you can see that there is the required instrument of faith to reach out and take hold of God. It is faith that looks unto the Spirit of God and cries out that God would make us holy, would sanctify us, would make us pure, and would cleanse us from our sins.

There is the need of faith, realizing that we cannot sanctify ourselves, realizing that God demands holiness of us, realizing that we are incapable of producing it. Therefore, we not only make use of the means of grace, but we trust in the Giver of grace and the Sanctifier of men who is the Holy Spirit of God.

Are you aware of your corruption? Does your heart cry out in anguish as you consider your inward disease? Are you growing in grace? Are you more faithful in your prayer life? If you would grow in sanctification, then make use of the means of grace. Start spending more time in prayer. Start seriously studying the Word of God. Determine that you are going to give yourself over to new obedience and walk in all of the ways of God's commandments. Many a Christian is determined that he is going to walk in part of the ways of God's commandments and thus he gets nowhere at all. Repentance requires determination after total new obedience on our part.

Would you know the holiness of God? Then you will have to know Him who is holy, for apart from Him, the thrice-holy God, there is nothing in this sin-tainted world but death and corruption. Draw near unto Him. Spend time unto Him. Reach out in faith unto Him. And you will come to know the blessings of God's holiness and the meaning of His sanctification.

O God, deliver us, we pray Thee, from a corrupted view of Thy holiness. May we never forget that Thou hast said, "Be ye holy, for I am holy . . . without holiness no man shall see God." For thou art the altogether holy one. O Lord, teach us to despise our sin and corruption, our vileness and rottenness, and may we reach unto Thee, O Thou Source of purity and holiness, that we may be healed and made whole in body, mind, and soul. We pray it in the name of Christ. *Amen.*

10 ADOPTION

For ye have not received the spirit of bondage again to fear; but ye have received the Spirit of adoption, whereby we cry, Abba, Father.

Romans 8:15

In the preceding chapters, we have seen how God revealed Himself through the Scriptures and ultimately in His Son. We have also seen the central Personage about whom this revelation speaks is the Triune God: Father, Son, and Holy Ghost. We have seen God to be infinitely sovereign, in control of all things in the world from the greatest to the smallest, and there is nothing that takes place which is not under His control. He firmly holds in His hands the reins of the world; kings and subjects do according to His bidding. Whether it be by His directive or His permissive decree, all things come to pass according to Him who has foreordained everything after the council of His own will.

We see that God, after determining to create the world, made man in a perfect, sinless state. He then placed him on probation and gave him one commandment which, if he kept, would have earned for himself and all mankind eternal blessedness, bliss, and peace forevermore. But man, because of his fallibility and out of his own will, chose to rebel against his Maker and thus plunged the whole human

Genesis 2, 3

race into sin and earned for his posterity, not life and peace, but death and misery.

God could have let man go his own way and allowed him to face judgment and punishment. But in His infinite mercy, God determined to show favor and grace to His creation and offered man eternal life. He foresaw, however, that this offer would be spurned by man for "there is none that seeketh after God . . . they have turned everyone to their own way." Left to himself, man's heart is at enmity with God. His mind neither understands nor appreciates the things of the Spirit.

Romans 3:11, 12

Therefore, God determined He would select from this mass of fallen mankind some whom He would determinately save. To this end, He predestinated a great mass of men out of every nation, tongue, and tribe to make them His sons. He not only invites them but He sends His Spirit to bring them irresistibly, invincibly, unfailingly, effectually unto Himself, renewing their hearts and minds, quickening them from the deadness of their sins, and bringing them to Christ. They come most willingly having been made willing by His grace.

Revelation 5:9

To provide this salvation for men, God gave His only begotten Son to die in their stead for their sins, to pay their transgressions, that God might show favor unto them and still remain the just Judge of all the earth. In His proper and appointed time, He sent forth His Holy Spirit to effectually call them, and by His Word and Spirit the dead sinner leaps to life, his mind is quickened, his soul renewed, his will changed and made malleable. After hearing God's voice and knock at the door, he says, "It is my Beloved; I will go and open unto Him." We see after being given faith by God as a gift, man is also justified on the basis of that very faith so all his salvation may be of grace. Salvation is of God. But the *Ordo salutis*, or the way of salvation as it is divinely revealed in the Scriptures, is not yet complete.

Colossians 4:3

In this chapter, I want to discuss one of the greatest doctrines of the Christian faith: The doctrine of adoption. This doctrine has been greatly neglected throughout church history. Luther had little to say about it and Calvin ignored it almost entirely. The great theologian Jean Alphonse Turretin confused it with the second part of justification wherein man is clothed with righteousness and made righteous in the sight of God. To be made righteous in the sight of the law is entirely different than to be received into the house of the Father. We find the well-known theologian Robert Lewis Dabney followed in the train of Turretin and made the same mistake. Even the great systematic theologian, Charles Hodge, omits it from the paragraph headings of his volumes. However, the Westminster Confession of Faith does contain a brief chapter on adoption.

Because it has been neglected, I think it is important that we rediscover this great doctrine. First, because it is of immeasurable solace to the saints of God when calamity overwhelms and tribulation comes in like a flood. What child of God has not turned to Him when losing a loved one? Is it not to our Father's home that our heart turns when this earthly tabernacle begins to crumble and dissolve? This is what adoption is all about.

It is also important because it is a biblical doctrine—the great end to the doctrine of predestination. We are predestinated that we might become the adopted children of God. It is the final consummation, the ultimate blessing, of the Christian life. It is also important because it is the theological point of contact with this century's greatest heresy.

It is said that every century has its own peculiar heresy and this century has not been found wanting. Universalism is a doctrine which is spreading and being proclaimed forcibly and eloquently from many pulpits across our land, even when the creeds of that church explicitly deny it. It is the doctrine that says somehow, somewhere, sometime, everyone of God's creatures will ultimately arrive in paradise. It is a doctrine which utterly denies and abhors the biblical doctrine of eternal punishment and rejects the scriptural teaching that man could forever be separated from God. Yet the Bible plainly teaches, and Christian churches believe, there will be those who will be forever separated form God. Jesus Christ Himself, the King of the Kingdom, made it plain: "Enter ye in at the strait gate: for wide is the gate, and broad is the way, that leadeth to destruction, and many there be which go in thereat: Because strait is the gate, and narrow is the way, which leadeth unto life, and few there be that find it."

Matthew 7:13, 14

The point at which universalism impinges upon the doctrine of adoption is what is called the "fatherhood of God and the brotherhood of man." I suppose many Christian people believe the doctrine of the fatherhood of God and the brotherhood of man to be biblical. This merely proves

Hitler's dictum: Tell a lie which is big enough, tell it loud enough and often enough, and you can get most people to believe it. This is just what Satan has done at this point and his success is notable. The concept of the universal fatherhood of God and universal brotherhood of man is utterly foreign to the Scriptures. It is only in the past fifty or seventy-five years that it has even been seen in theological writings. It is an utterly foreign doctrine to older biblical scholars because it is completely foreign to the Bible.

John 8:44

Ephesians 2:2

Jesus said: "Ye are of your father the devil and his works do ye do." Paul says we were "children of disobedience." This is the state of the natural man as he is born into this world. He is a disobedient child of the devil, under the wrath of God. One family with one Father? Not at all! We must be translated out of the kingdom of darkness into the Kingdom of God's dear Son. All sons of God? Listen: "But as many as received him [Christ], to them gave he power to become the sons of God . . . ."

John 1:12

How can one become something he already is? Of course he cannot. ". . . They which are children of the flesh, these are not the children of God: but the children of the promise are counted for the seed." "Wherefore come out from among them . . . [I] will be a Father unto you, and ye shall be my sons and daughters . . . ." No, the deception of the devil may be that all people are the sons of God and He is Father of all, but this is not the teaching of the Scriptures.

Romans 9:8

2 Corinthians 6:17, 18

To be perfectly accurate let me point out the term *sons of God* is used in Scripture three ways. First, when God originally made man, he was the son of God. This is his lowest concept. (That condition was utterly obliterated, as we shall see.) Second, there is the adoptive sense of all believers. "For ye are all sons of God by faith in Jesus Christ." It is only those who have faith in Jesus Christ who are the sons of God. And finally, in its restrictive, single, unique sense, it refers to the Son of God, Jesus Christ Himself, who is the eternal second Person of the Trinity and has forever been the Son of God.

John 1:12

Let us look at the beginning and see what happened. God made Adam as His son—perfect, without sin. But Adam was not only the son of God, he was also the subject of God and stood before God in both of these relationships. If we want to understand biblical theology, it is important to understand that Adam was not only *son* but also *subject*.

He was a member of the divine Kingdom but also of the divine household. God, to him, was Sovereign and Lord; He was also Father and Friend. Adam was placed under probation in both of these relationships, both as a citizen of the Kingdom and as a son of the Father. If he had obeyed, we would all have had an eternal citizenship in the Kingdom of God and eternal sonship in the House of God. But rather, he sinned against the magisterial favor of the King and against the paternal regard of his Father. In one act, he sinned both ways. The result was spiritual death. This means that as a citizen he was outlawed and as a son banished and disinherited. Therefore, all his children (each one of us born into this world) are born under the scowl of a righteous Judge and the frown of a benevolent Father.

This is man's condition. It is described succinctly by Dr. Robert Webb, who said concerning Adam and all of his natural children after their sin: "There was, there could be, there ought to have been, but one denouement to such a situation—a child with a heart so perverted ought to have been excluded. God dismissed him. Today he has neither the right nor spirit of a child. He is legally disowned because he is morally bad. He is ungoverned, because he is ungovernable. He has thrown off his Father's authority, because he has cast away his Father's disposition. Moral gravitation has naturally and logically carried him into that fellowship where the outraged sensibilities of his Father have justly consigned him. Parental discipline has dealt with him according to the demands and desires of his own degenerate nature. He has been permitted to have his wilful way; and the misery of his course will be the just retribution of his heady and impertinent career. He is a child of Satan; therefore a 'child of wrath.' "

Now what does man need? He needs a twofold remedy for his condition. The exact status of fallen man is a *proscribed citizen* and a *disinherited child*. It means he must be restored to his legal citizenship in the Kingdom of God and must be recovered into the bosom and household of his Father. This is his problem. What is its solution? This double solution is clearly stated in Scripture. On one hand, his problem of citizenship is dealt with by the doctrine of justification. In justification, the transgressed law of God is fulfilled by Christ and the penalty paid by Him. The sinner is clothed in the righteousness of Christ and restored to the Kingdom of God. His sonship is taken care of in the doctrine of adoption whereby he is adopted into the family of God and restored to His household.

When we look more closely at the doctrine of adoption, we notice it has some relation to the doctrine of justification. We also note it has a relation to the doctrine of regeneration because the problem of adoption is twofold. Not only must the child be restored to the filial position but also be restored to a filial disposition. He must be given a filial nature, the nature of a child, because the natural man has a despiteful attitude towards his parents. It is the attitude of a teen-ager who says to his parents, "I hate you; I never want to lay eyes on you again. I couldn't care less what you have done for me." But when such a person is regenerated by faith in Christ, he is given a new heart and nature and is restored to the rights and privileges of the household of God. This is done by adoption.

Let us look carefully at the theology of the fatherhood of God and the brotherhood of man. Also let me state again that this is a new religion which is foreign to the historic religion of Jesus Christ. It's a religion of paternalism. I think it's interesting that universalism should rise in the twentieth century when we see the same thing happening in government. People want a paternalistic government and a paternalistic religion where they believe God is just naturally the Father of everyone. Such people say God created people because He was lonely. They fail to realize that God is the absolute perfect Person; the three Persons of the Triune God have never been lonely. God did not create man because He was lonely; He created man for His own glory. They also fail to understand the difference between divine government and divine discipline; between the ruling of a Sovereign, and the ruling of a Father.

And what are these differences? They are seen in many ways. For example, a sovereign-state ruler exercises justice and punishes the rebellious citizen, the transgressor of the law. A father operates on the basis of love and chastens rather than punishes his child.

The difference between punishment and chastisement is great. Punishment is retrospective—it looks backward to the broken law and is not done to make the criminal better. Rather it's done because the transgressed law demands punishment. Chastisement is prospective—it looks to the future. It's not given for a broken law but for the presence of a fault. It's to make the child better. An electric chair never made anyone better. It may make society better since one of the reasons for justice is the protection of society; but the reason for chastening is to make a better child.

Further, the universalist denies the need of an atonement and reduces the Bible to the story of the prodigal son, where the father embraces the son without atonement or payment for his sins. But you see, that's the nature of fatherly discipline. All the father requires is repentance and evidence of a desire to do better in the future. So these people suppose this to be the way of salvation. They believe if a person merely repents and evidences that he will do better in the future, all will be well.

This is to suppose that a murderer given a life sentence could, after two days in jail, rattle the bars and say to the warden: "Warden, I've had a change of heart. You'll be delighted to know I'm sorry about the whole thing. I've decided I shouldn't have killed all those people. It just wasn't the right thing to do. Please tell the jailer to open the cage and let me out because I'll never do that again." There's a difference between fatherly discipline, the practice of justice, and the penalty of the law!

The universalist, therefore, fails to understand that God not only makes man a member of His Kingdom, but also adopts him into His family. Both of these are found in Jesus Christ who came not only as Servant but also as Son. Jesus as the suffering Servant is subject to the King; obedient to God in all His ways. Jesus pays the penalty as the Servant and thus God restores Him to His legal citizenship in the Kingdom. Jesus is also the very Son of God because it takes the Son by filial obedience to restore the sinful, disobedient son to a filial relation. And so Christ, the suffering Servant and suffering Son, comes and provides for us not only our justification and restoration to the Kingdom of God, but also our adoption and reclamation into the very family of God. This is the great biblical doctrine of adoption.

We are brought into the family of God, given His name, and made heirs by an act of God's grace. We also have the promise that we have His spirit put within us; He pities us as a Father, provides for all our needs, watches over us, defends us from our enemies, and one day will take us to that mansion in glory which He has prepared for us.

How wonderful it is that because of the Spirit of Adoption we can look up into the face of God, whom many fear, and say, "Abba, Father."

Romans 8:15

I once pointed out to a Jehovah's Witness that their *New World Translation* of the Scripture was not correct in including, in the New Testament, scores of times the word *Jehovah* which does not one time appear in the Greek text of the New Testament. This person responded by asking, "Why would God not use His Name in the New Testament?" I cannot answer for God. Though I cannot for sure say why He did not do it, I can for certain state that He *did not* do it. I do have an idea, however, as to what the reason might be. Let me explain it by this story. When our little girl, Jennifer, was about five years old, she passed through a phase where she began to call her mother and me by our first names—Anne and Jim (since she had heard others do this). After a few weeks of this, I sat her on my knee and said to her, "Jennifer, darling, there are thousands of people in this world who can call me Jim, but there is no other person on this earth who can call me 'Daddy,' except you and to you, Jennifer, my name is—Daddy!"

So also God revealed His Name in the Old Testament as Jehovah—The Ever-Living One. But in the New Testament, when we are given the spirit of adoption and brought into that intimate relationship of sons of God, we can look up into the face of our Father and say, "Abba," which is a diminutive of the Aramaic word for father and means, essentially—Daddy!

Are you a child of God? Have you come to the place of receiving Jesus Christ? Can you say, "I'm a child of the King"?

John 1:12

"But as many as received him [Christ], to them gave he power to become the sons of God." Beloved now are we the children of God. In Jesus name. *Amen.*

11 ASSURANCE OF SALVATION

These things have I written unto you that believe on the name of
the Son of God; that ye may know that ye have eternal life, and
that ye may believe on the name of the Son of God.

1 John 5:13

Not long ago a radio announcer in Chicago took a survey
in a train station. He asked about twenty-five or thirty
people if they knew for sure that they were going to heaven.
The result was interesting—a unanimous no. In fact, several became indignant and said: "Nobody can know such a
thing as that!"

Contrast this with the statement by the great scientist, Sir
Michael Faraday, discoverer of magnetism, who on his
deathbed was asked: "What speculations do you have
about life after death?"

"Speculations!" he replied in astonishment. "Why I have
no speculations! I'm resting on certainties! I know whom
I have believed, and am persuaded that He is able to keep
that which I have committed unto Him against that day."

This certainty of heaven is not only the possession of the
great and wise of the world, but also the poor and humble.
An elderly Scottish woman who lay at death's door was
visited by her pastor. "Sadie," he said, "suppose when you
die God should allow you to perish. What then?"

John 11:26

"Well," she said, "that's up to Him. He will do what He will. But if He does allow me to perish, He will lose more than I; for though I will lose my soul, He will lose His honor, for He has promised me in His Word, '[He that] believeth in me shall never die.' "

An old fisherman, who lived by the sea, was asked by a friend if he still believed he was going to heaven. "Look out the window," said the fisherman. "Are the seven great stones still there?"

"Yes," said his friend.

"Is the old mountain crag there?"

"Yes," came the reply.

"Well," said the fisherman, "the mountains shall disappear and the hills shall be cast down, but My Word shall last forever."

1 Peter 1:25

The Bible makes it plain that we can know what will become of us. But why is it that so many people today, in and out of church, do not know they are on their way to heaven? Because they *are not* on their way to heaven! Indeed it would be strange if God put the assurance into the heart of a person that he was on his way to heaven when in fact he was hastening into hell.

This was brought out in a radio survey when the reporter asked people on what they based their hope of heaven. Without exception they said: "Myself, my efforts, striving, church-going, goodness, character, morality, commandment-keeping." No wonder they don't know or have the assurance, because these answers are the very antithesis of Christianity. Everyone who is going to heaven *knows* he is. Are you going there?

A few weeks ago I received a call from a young lady who was deeply perplexed. She had been going to a church whose modern minister was well informed about current events but evidently quite uninformed about the eternal verities of the Word of God. He had completely confused her to the point where she didn't know where she was going or why. He declared that nobody could know they were going to heaven and it was impossible for anyone to have a sudden or instantaneous conversion. "Salvation," he said, "is a long process and not something you can have overnight."

"What kind of a church is this?" I asked.

"A Protestant church," she said.

"Well," I said, "I recommend this minister go back and

check the foundations of Protestantism and examine its taproot."

I suggested he look at the life of Martin Luther who struggled for years to earn his salvation. Finally on his knees crawling up the *sancta scala* (sacred stairs) in Rome, while reciting his mumbled prayers, was suddenly struck with the words: "The just shall live by faith!" We are justified by faith—not all these vain works! With the assurance of eternal life flooding his heart, Luther began the Protestant Reformation.

Romans 1:17

Consider John Calvin, the founder of the Presbyterian and Reformed branches of the Protestant world, who relates his conversion in one sentence: "God *suddenly converted* me unto Himself."

John Wesley, founder of the Methodist Church, said in his diary: "It was a quarter to nine and for the first time in my life I knew that I trusted Jesus Christ alone for my salvation. I felt my heart strangely warmed and *knew* that He had delivered me from sin and death unto eternal life." He didn't name the year, month, week, day, or hour—he named the *minute!* It was a quarter to nine! He came to know in a moment!

I told the young lady the minister's denials were not peripheral matters but struck at the very heart of the gospel. They were perverting the Christian faith.

The Bible says eternal life is a free gift from God. It is unearned, unworked for, unstriven for, unmerited, undeserved. It's a gift completely paid for by Christ and offered by His free grace. Then how long does it take to obtain this gift? You merely reach out and take it. "He [Jesus] came unto his own, and his own received him not. But as many as received him, to them *gave* he power to *become* the sons of God . . . ." Eternal life is a gift that is received in an instant.

John 1:11, 12

Did you receive a gift last Christmas? Did it take you twenty years to get it? Do you know whether or not you have it? So it is with eternal life! It is the greatest Christmas present God has ever given to the world. ". . . *The gift of God is eternal life through Jesus Christ our Lord.*"

Romans 6:23

The essence of Protestantism says: Heaven is free and therefore we may know we have it. The Protestant faith does not keep men in fear of what will happen to them when they die. That is the essence of Romanism. The Council of Trent of the Roman Church says: "Let that man

1 John 5:13

2 Peter 1:10

2 Peter 1:10
John 20:31
1 John 3:14

Job 19:25

2 Timothy 1:12

Philippians 4:4

who says he knows he has eternal life be anathema." But the Word of God says: "These things are written that you may *know* that ye have eternal life." The Bible not only says you *can* know it but *commands* you to know it: "Make your calling and election *sure*." This is not advice, this is a commandment. Every day you fail to do that, you are sinning against God by breaking this commandment. "Make your calling and election *sure* . . . ." "These things are written that ye might [*know*] . . . ." "We ye *know* that we have passed from death unto life . . . ."

No, the Bible doesn't deal with question marks. The faith of the Bible is a stirring exclamation point! "For I know that my redeemer liveth." ". . . I know whom I have believed, and am persuaded that he is able to keep that which I have committed unto him against that day." There is joy in such knowledge like nothing else can bring, because this assurance is the source of Christian joy. It is this kind of joy in our souls that puts spring in our steps and makes us sing songs as we walk down the street.

It was this joy that enabled blind Fanny Crosby to write: "Blessed assurance, Jesus is mine, O what a foretaste of glory divine!" No wonder many don't smile when they sing such a song. They are spiritually blind to the great truth it teaches! It is paganism which fills the heart with dark, doubting fear when death approaches. Christianity is a religion of assurance, faith, confidence, joy. The reason a Christian can rejoice is because he knows he is going to heaven. The Apostle Paul says, "Rejoice . . . and again I say, Rejoice."

His heart burdened with sin, Charles Spurgeon tells of his searching for God as a young lad in London. For five years, he wandered from place to place seeking someone who could give him a word of assurance. He said he did not so much fear the wrath of God as he feared sin itself for what it was. He said, "If some preacher had told me to bare my back and with fifty lashes would earn eternal life, I would have instantly ripped the shirt from my back and said, 'Do your worst. Spare not the rod if it will bring peace to my troubled soul.' If they had told me to run a hundred miles barefooted, I would have started off immediately, if I could have gained eternal life. But to trust in Christ, rest upon His finished work, simply by faith take hold of Him, do nothing except believe and receive, this I knew not how to get hold of at all."

Then one day, when he was but sixteen and a half, still bound by sin, Spurgeon wandered into a little chapel. There were only twelve or fifteen people present. The regular minister was gone and an uneducated, unlettered layman got up to speak. He chose for his text these words: "Look unto me, and be ye saved, all the ends of the earth . . . ." He began in the simplest language: "There's not a hand that's lifted or a foot that's moved; there's not a thing that's done. Only a look, because there's life for a look at the Crucified One. The problem with many is that they look to themselves. As long as you look within yourself, you will never find the secret of salvation. 'Look unto Me,' says Christ. Not unto God the Father—that will come later; not unto the Holy Spirit—look unto Jesus who came from glory and died for our sins."

Isaiah 45:22

Suddenly the layman stopped, looked down, and saw young Charles Spurgeon. Pointing his finger at him, he said: "Young man, you're miserable. Further, you are going to be miserable forever unless you obey my text: Look unto Christ."

"And," said Spurgeon years later, "in that moment my soul was flooded with the reality of the grace of God. I looked unto the cross of Jesus Christ and saw there His hands pierced for my sins; I saw Him bearing the burden of my guilt upon His back; I saw the wrath of God that I deserved falling upon Him. Suddenly I realized that *it was finished!* It was done, the payment made, it was over, and I knew I had received eternal life. My soul was filled with joy. I could have danced all the way home. I could not restrain myself but to tell another one of the Jesus, blessed Jesus, whom I had found and who had found me."

Do you have that blessed assurance? It is the wellspring of all Christian motives for holy living. Unless you know you have eternal life, everything you have ever done for Christ has been a sin. I repeat: Unless you know that you have eternal life, everything you have ever done for Christ has been a sin—because your *motive* was wrong! If you don't know you *have* eternal life, everything you are doing is an effort to *get* eternal life, and thus your motive is gain and greed. But God in His mercy came down, incarnate in Christ, died on the cross, and paid for our sins, purchased for us eternal life, and by His graciousness offers it freely to us as a gift. Faith is but the hand of a beggar reaching out to receive the gift of a King. The motive then for Christian living is not gain, but *gratitude* for the gift of eternal life. God begins by giving us everything!

Have you received eternal life? Or is death still for you an uncertainty—a leap into outer darkness? If so, I assure you it will be just that: outer, eternal darkness, where there will be weeping and wailing and gnashing of teeth. But you *can know*. That doubt can be changed to singing and certainty that will bring forth joy and peace. Would you receive the gift He offers you? Would you take Him at His Word? ". . . He that believeth not God hath made him a liar; because he believeth not the record that God gave of his Son. This is the record, that God hath given to us eternal life, and this life is in his Son. He that hath the Son hath life . . . ." Do you believe it? Have you received it? Have you invited the Son to come into your life as Saviour, Master, and Lord? "He that believeth on the Son of God hath the witness in himself . . . ." "The [Holy] Spirit itself beareth witness with our spirit, that we are the children of God."

1 John 5:10–12

1 John 5:10

Romans 8:16

And then, if you have done that, you can sing with real meaning: "*Blessed assurance,* Jesus is *mine,* O what a foretaste of glory divine." *Amen.*

12 GOOD WORKS

"For by grace are ye saved through faith; and that not of your-selves: it is the gift of God: Not of works, lest any man should boast." Those words are familiar to most of us. But are we as familiar with the following verse: *"For we are his workman-ship, created in Christ Jesus unto good works, which God hath before ordained that we should walk in them."*

Ephesians 2:8–10

In this chapter, I want to discuss the place of good works in the scheme of Christian theology. Is man redeemed by his own works? Are we required to do them and do we have any?

As believers in Christ, we have been set apart or sanc-tified unto good works. From this, we see sanctification is essentially the mortification of the old man and the creation of the new. In discussing the work of sanctification in producing good works, we must remember sanctification is the work of God the Holy Spirit within us. Sanctifiction is creating a new nature, a new heart, a holy disposition. The ground soil of our own character, of our souls, is changed and holiness is implanted within us. Good works, on the other hand, is something done by us. "This is a faithful saying, and these things I will that thou affirm constantly, that they which have believed in God might be careful to maintain good works."

2 Timothy 2:21

Titus 3:8

While the work of Christ is vicarious, the work of the Holy Spirit is not. Christ does something for us, in our stead, in our place, as our substitute. He died in our place on the cross. The hope of our salvation is based upon the vicarious substitutionary work of Jesus Christ in our stead. The work of the Holy Spirit is not. He does not do something for us; He works in us. His work can never be counted as our own. He creates something within us and He stirs us up to do something in response to that. This something which we do is called *good works*. Sanctification is something imparted to us. Good works are something taken from us.

Now what is a *good work*? There are three requirements of any work before it can be called *good* in the biblical sense. The first most obvious is one which many people seem unable to grasp. What is the most basic thing required of a work for it to be good? I have asked this question to dozens of people including classes of elders and deacons I have taught. I had all sorts of answers, but the simplest and most obvious always eludes them. The first requirement for a work to be good is that it be commanded by God; that it be comformable to divine law. No matter how holy or zealous our inclinations when we decide to do something for God, if He has not commanded us to do it, then the good work is not pleasing to God. God says: "Who has commanded thee to do these things?"

Acts 5:38

Religions through the centuries have commanded people to do all sorts of human works which they invented as supposedly pleasing to God. But the only way to please God is to obey Him.

Philosophers have invented schemes to determine what is good. John Stuart Mills's famous definition was: "That which does the greatest good to the greatest number." This is called utilitarianism but it is not always true. Hitler was a utilitarian. Furthermore, it's often completely impossible to determine what will do the greatest good to the greatest number. The Communists are sure they are doing the greatest good to the greatest number when they kill millions of people to make way for Communism.

Some say: Good is the thing which brings me the greatest pleasure. Others have said good is that which is expedient and, if it seems to be expedient, it's good. There are others who say good is what they have learned from grandpa. It's amazing how many ethical standards have been handed down from Aunt Susie, mom and dad, grandma and grandad. "As old granddaddy used to say . . . . Now that's what I believe and that's what I do . . . ." It doesn't matter that the Word of God contradicts it. Granddaddy did it that way and that's the way it's going to be! This is making a god out of our grandparent. Every opinion of men must come under the scrutiny of God's Word. Only God, the absolute Lawgiver and Creator of this world, can determine what is good.

Therefore, we can begin by saying the good man is the obedient man. People say, "Oh, he was such a good man. Of course he didn't go to church, read the Bible, or pray. He didn't do this or that . . . but he was a good man." That is not true! If he is a disobedient man by the biblical definition of that which is good, he is not a good man. A good man must first become the obedient man—obedient to the will of God—and the holy law of God is the divine transcript of the immutable and eternal will of God. Furthermore, the good man obeys out of love for God. "If ye love me, keep my commandments."

John 14:15

The first aspect of a good work then is something God has commanded us to do. Don't worry about this, because God's law, which rises up out of the trunk of God's basic will, branches off into the ten branches of the Ten Commandments and then contains thousands of boughs, smaller branches, and leaves, covering all aspects of human conduct. God has told us clearly in His Word what He wants us to do. Never in this life will we get through doing what He has told us to do, much less have to invent something He didn't tell us to do.

I am amazed at people who suppose a Christian is to have nothing to do with the law of God. This antinomian (against the law) teaching has clung to the church like a cancer for centuries but is completely contrary to God's Word. Jesus Christ fulfilled the law as a covenant of works and took the penalty of it, but the law of God still remains the only transcript of the immutable will of God. "He that hath my commandments, and keepeth them, he it is that loveth me."

John 14:21

The second requirement for a work to be good is that it must be done from a heart purified by faith. Any work considered hypothetically by itself (for example giving a thousand dollars to the poor) is one thing; but considered in relation to the motive, object, or end of the person doing it, is another. We see it's possible for a person to do tens of thousands of things which God commands him to do without ever having done a single good work—because the good work must first come from a heart purified by faith. Jesus makes this most explicit when He says "An evil tree brings forth evil fruit and a corrupt tree cannot bring forth good fruit." It is impossible for the human heart in its natural, depraved, sinful state to ever bring forth anything which in the sight of God would be considered good.

The human heart must be purified by faith because, ". . . without faith it is impossible to please [God]." Faith is that which lays hold of the justifying and sanctifying grace of God. Faith brings the Holy Spirit into the heart to cleanse, wash, purify, and work within us those holy inclinations and dispositions to do things which are truly pleasing to a Holy God. Without the cleansing of the stream at its source, it can never bring forth pure water. A bitter fountain cannot bring forth sweet waters any more than a corrupt tree can bring forth good fruit. What does this mean? It means the unregenerate man (human beings as they are born into the world before receiving Jesus Christ as their Saviour and before the Holy Spirit has created a holy state within them) can only bring forth evil fruit until God changes his heart.

Therefore, the reason the unregenerate person cannot get to heaven by his good works is not because he does not have *enough,* but because he doesn't have *any!* ". . . For whatsoever is not of faith is sin."

The Bible says the "plowing of the wicked, is sin." Consider that devastating statement! This means a non-Christian farmer who rises before sunrise and goes about his duties, working in the fields while the blazing sun beats down upon his perspiring back, is sinning in the sight of God. Why? Because, even though God commanded man should work with his hands and earn his daily bread, his motive for working does not proceed from a heart which has been cleansed and made holy. Therefore, his work is sin.

The same situation would apply to pirates who infested the islands off the Florida coast. A search into their activities might reveal many commendable things in the eyes of men. They might have been nice to their wives and cared for their children. They might have been generous and worked diligently at their boats. They might have worked

Matthew 7:18

Hebrews 11:6

Romans 14:23
Proverbs 21:4

hard to plant and raise crops. Yet every seed they planted, every ear of corn they harvested, was part of the effort to gain more food, to gather more strength, to continue their willful rebellion against the authority of the United States! Therefore, they were guilty and the government could only ask them to surrender.

So the plowing of the wicked man is merely an effort to gain food, to gain strength, to continue his willful rebellion against the rightful sovereign authority of Jesus Christ. There are church members who diligently work or study, yet everything they do is sin because they are gathering more strength to continue their rebellion against Almighty God who commands us to lay down our arms and surrender to Him. A good work must proceed from a purified source—a heart cleansed by faith with a true love of God.

Not only must a good work be something which is commanded by God in His Word and come from a purified heart, but it must also be done to the right end. This is the third and last aspect of a good work.

At a "Men of the Church" picnic, one of the gentlemen brought a magnificent archery set. I've never seen anything like it, not because I'm completely unfamiliar with the sport, because I used to enjoy it. (Before we were married I bought my future wife just what any young lady's heart would most desire—two archery sets! Do you think my motive was right?) The set was beautiful—marvelous arrows, straight, polished, and strong. But regardless of how magnificent the bow, how strongly bent, how straight and powerful the arrow, it would avail nothing at all unless the aim were right.

Do you see the point? It makes no difference how beautiful a deed may be in itself. It makes no difference how highly polished, how magnificent and extraordinary, how much effort and energy goes into the work, if its direction is not right, it matters not at all and the work is not good; it is sin.

Suppose, while admiring the archery set, I had picked up the bow and arrow and accidentally shot it into the heart of one of my friends. This thing of beauty now becomes an object of horror—an instrument of death! Unless our works are directed toward the glory of God, they are not good!

What is the chief end of man? What is the purpose for man's existence? Why are we here? What are we supposed to do? What is the chief function of a can opener? It's to

open cans! We once had a can opener that was very attrac-
tive. It had intricate gears that would go around and
around, but it wouldn't open a can! And you know what
happened to it? The garbage can! That's exactly what God
says will happen to us. God made us for His own glory and,
if we become useless and do not fulfill the things for which
we are made, then we will end up in what He calls Gehenna
of fire—the garbage heap of Jerusalem. We shall go away
into eternal fire.

Matthew 3:10

The chief end of man is to glorify God and to enjoy Him
forever. ". . . At thy right hand there are pleasures and
joys for evermore." We are to enjoy and glorify God. The
end of all our actions is to be the glory of God. The con-
scious, thoughtful, purposeful, directed end of our actions
is always the glory of God and any action which falls short
of that glory is thereby not a good work and is sin. Abraham
Kuyper says that the intention, direction, and aim of the
heart is *everything* in what we do. The end and aim of all
things must be the Lord God alone. We were created to
glorify Him and everything we do, regardless of what the
proximate aim may be, the ultimate aim must be the glory
of God.

Psalms 16:11

We talk about self-denial, but the true biblical concept of
self-denial is to completely deny self not only in respect to
men, but also in respect to God; to deny pointing our good
deeds back to ourselves; deny seeking the praise of men for
ourselves. Jesus condemned them saying: "Ye seek the
praise of men rather than the praise of God."

John 12:43

A young man once told me he couldn't see anything
wrong with a person going out for his life's goal, to seek to
be successful, make a name for himself, be famous, and
make money. But God says the essence of sin is for man to
put himself in God's place and direct all his glory at his own
ego, at his own self. Satan said: "I will lift up myself into the
place of God."

Abraham Kuyper illustrated this by saying that on every
ship there is a small unseen object which controls its
destination—the rudder. It doesn't matter how
magnificently rigged may be the schooner, how full the
sails, how rich and precious the cargo, or how streamlined
the hull; unless the rudder directs the ship to its destination, it will end up upon the rocks of disaster.

So it is with our good works. Down beneath the waves of
our lives, unseen by other men, is a rudder that directs all

we do. It directs our works to the glory of God or turns them back to the glory of ourselves. We seek the end of God's glory and magnificence or the end of our own advancement and praise among men. It matters not how fully rigged and magnificent may be the good works of our life, or how precious the cargo of seemingly good works we carry, it's the rudder that makes the difference.

The great cry of the Protestant Reformation was *Soli deo gloria*—solely for the glory of God. Thus every action of man must be solely for the glory of God. We are to win men to Jesus Christ not merely that they may be saved or for us to be obedient; rather that the glory of the majestic mercy of God may appear. These only are good works.

Again my question: Do you have a good work? How foolish for the unregenerate to believe he can buy eternal life and earn his way to heaven. Are we saved by these good works? Evidently not, because until we are saved we do not possess one good work. "We are . . . created in Christ Jesus *unto good works.*" It is "Not of works, lest any man should boast." It's a matter of the cart and horse. "Therefore by the deeds of the law there shall no flesh be justified in his sight." We are saved by faith in Jesus Christ alone —nothing else!

Ephesians 2:10
Ephesians 2:9, 10

Romans 3:20

Are good works necessary to salvation? The answer is *yes, they are.* They are the necessary consequence of our salvation. This is not only the answer of Scripture but that of the apostolic fathers and Reformers (Luther, Calvin, Knox). It is the answer of the statements of all the great Protestant churches. It is the statement of the Westminster Confession of Faith. It is the Word of God: "Even so faith, if it hath not works, is dead [vain, empty, meaningless, nonexistent]." As Martin Luther said: "People talk about being saved by faith plus good works. This is not true. Good works are the necessary consequence of our salvation. They are not necessary to be saved; they are the necessary result of our salvation and the evidence that we truly have faith." You could no more have faith without good works than you could have lightning without thunder, or fire without heat. If we have a saving faith, we will inevitably have good works.

James 2:17

Luther also said that this faith is a divine work within us. It begets us anew. It creates us as new men and new creatures and all the various faculties of our being, and is constantly engaged in good works. It does not wait till the question should be asked, but, before the question is asked, it has done them and is constantly engaged in doing them and he who does not do such good works is a man without faith.

The Westminster Confession of Faith says that we are justified by faith alone. This faith which justifies is never alone in the individual who is justified, but is always accompanied by the fruits which this produces in the life. Faith in Christ produces a life of good works. Therefore, those people who make a profession of faith and then sit down and do nothing for God, who have no service or good works for the Lord, vainly deceive themselves of being in a state of salvation and in God's favor—which hope shall perish with them!

Good works are absolutely the necessary result of a saving faith and are the *only evidence* of it. "For by grace are ye saved through faith; and that not of yourselves: it is the gift of God: Not of works, lest any man should boast. For we are his workmanship, created in Christ Jesus unto good works, which God hath before ordained that we should walk in them."

Ephesians 2:8–10

O God, may we prove our faith by our works. May we examine our hearts. May Your glory be ever before us as our aim and goal. May all we do be done to Your glory and praise. We ask it in Thy blessed name, who, with the Father and the Holy Spirit, are the eternal and most Holy God, now and forevermore. *Amen.*

13 PERSEVERANCE OF THE SAINTS

Moreover whom he did predestinate, them he also called: and whom he called, them he also justified: and whom he justified, them he also glorified.

Romans 8:30

The question with which I would like to engage your thinking is: *Can a Christian cease to be a Christian,* or, as it might be otherwise stated, *can a person who has been saved ever be lost?* Can a person who has been regenerated ever become unregenerated? Can one who has been translated into the Kingdom of God's dear Son be translated back into the kingdom and family of the devil? Can a person receive eternal life and then go to hell forever? This is an important question because it has to do with a very important aspect of our lives and speaks concerning our eternal welfare.

Let us look at the question historically and see what others have said about it. We might begin with the Roman Catholic Church. Their answer to this is *yes,* a person may be a Christian and then cease to be one; they may be saved and then be lost. Let us look next at the Lutheran Church for their answer. The Lutherans reply that a person may be saved and then may be lost. How about the group whose theology is known as Arminianism (the

Methodist Church being the largest representative, as well as others such as the Holiness and Pentecostal Churches)? Their answer to this question is an emphatic *yes*, a person may be saved and then lost.

What answer is given by the Calvinist to the question *can a person be saved and then lost?* To that question the Calvinist says *no.* Here we have a distinct tenet of the Calvinistic faith for virtually all others have said that it is possible to be lost after having once been saved. Therefore, it is important for us to examine this carefully.

The doctrine of the perseverance of the saints is a doctrine which only the Calvinist in history has acknowledged and which virtually all others have denied. I might point out to you that Calvinism is far broader than the Presbyterian Church as such, and there are other denominations who would be classified historically as holding to the Calvinist faith. They would include historically all of the reformed churches. The Anglican Church of England was historically Calvinistic, the Baptist Church was entirely Calvinistic, and to begin with the Congregational Churches were all Calvinistic.

Many of these churches, however, have thrown out some of their beliefs and no longer hold to the Calvinistic faith but have gone over to that other doctrinal viewpoint which is widely held in Protestantism, namely Arminianism. According to this view a person may be saved and then lost, and then saved again, and lost again, and this may happen hundreds of times until a person finally dies. Then the question is: *In which condition did he die?* In which state was his soul the moment that he passed from this world, as this will determine where he went?

Let us now note very carefully the matter of definition of that about which we are talking. I think it would also be well to notice what we are *not* talking about. If a person doesn't understand what grace is, they are not going to understand what perseverance in grace is. If they do not know what a saint is, they are hardly going to understand the perseverance of the saints. Those who are not Christians suppose that eternal life is something which is to be gained by their striving to live a good life. They do not have eternal life; therefore, they have nothing that they could lose except the possibility of getting it. These people do not understand that the Bible teaches salvation by grace as a gift of God by faith in Jesus Christ. What we are not talking about is a person trying to live a good life in order to get eternal life. That is not Christianity in any of its forms. Since eternal life is a gift and is freely given by God's grace to those who will trust in the Saviour, we are talking about whether God will give us the gift of eternal life and then take it back.

I spoke this week with a man who received Christ as his Saviour and received the gift of eternal life. One of his first comments was, "Well, I hope that three weeks from now I'm still a Christian." Would God give him eternal life and then take it back? The Bible says, "For the gifts and calling of God are without repentance." His gift of eternal life and his grace and his calling unto salvation are not repented of by God.

Romans 11:29

Some people have thought this doctrine means that a person can profess faith in Christ, then live any way he wants, and forty years later die and go to heaven. Not at all! The name of this doctrine is the *perseverance of the saints*. It has been called many things by other groups such as *eternal security, once saved—always saved*. However, I think that the true theological name is the best for it is very carefully formulated. It is the perseverance of the saints. It is not the preservation of the professers of religion, but the perseverance of the saints.

You will notice it is talking about saints, about those who have been sanctified by God (those who are His own). The Westminster Confession states it very succinctly in these words: "They whom God hath accepted in His beloved, effectually called and sanctified by His spirit, can neither totally nor finally fall away from the state of grace but shall certainly persevere therein to the end, and be eternally saved." It is those who have been regenerated by God and called by the Spirit and sanctified and accepted in the Beloved. It is speaking about those who are truly regenerated.

Notice it talks about their perseverance. The Bible says he that perseveres until the end shall be saved. It doesn't mean that we make a profession and then live for the world, the flesh, and the devil for years and then go to heaven. Only those who persevere till the end are those who are going to go to heaven.

Ephesians 6:18

The question is: *Will we persevere to the end?* There is no question about the fact that those who do not persevere to the end will *not* be saved. But can we persevere? Can we hold out? I am reminded of the alcoholic who for about the fiftieth time was signing the pledge to give up drinking and someone said to him, "Now this time sign it and keep it!" And he said, "Keep it? Man, I need somebody to keep me!" This has been the cry of many a heart who knows its weakness and its frailty. We need someone to keep us. Thank God there is such a One. The Bible says, "[We are kept through] the power of God unto salvation." The very omnipotent power of God keeps us and holds us in this salvation. If it were not for that none of us would persevere for one day. This should not lead to any pride, for the true Christian knows very clearly how weak he is. It is not that we have any strength in ourselves, but that we will be helped by God and enabled by God.

Romans 1:16

Might I point out to you that unless a person believes in the perseverance of the saints he cannot know that he is going to heaven. He may know that he is presently in a state of grace but he has no way of knowing that tomorrow he might fall from that state of grace and utterly perish. Therefore, it is only those who hold to this Calvinistic and biblical doctrine who can say, "I know I'm on my way to heaven." There are many in these various communions that I previously mentioned who (though officially their churches don't believe in this) as Christians have rejoiced in their hearts that they have eternal life and that Christ will never let them go.

Can you say, "I know that I'm going to heaven"? Do you know that you are saved? Of course these are two different questions. Can you say, "I know that I have eternal life; I know that I'm in a state of grace"? If you cannot then the subject we are discussing is of no value to you. You must first repent of your sins, cease to trust in your own good works, in your own strivings, and put your trust in Christ alone for your salvation. Then you can say, "I know that I'm in a state of grace. I know that I am forgiven." Then you can also come to claim God's promise that He will keep that which you have committed unto Him against that day.

We noted that a person may partially and temporarily fall away though not totally and finally. There are many examples of this not only in the lives of those in Scripture but in church history. Peter fell egregiously into sin; he denied his Lord; he blasphemed. But because of the seed of God in his heart, because of the eternal covenant of grace, because God was holding him by the hand, because He had sworn that He would not forsake him, because he was sealed by the Holy Spirit, he was brought back and became a faithful servant, though he partially and temporarily fell away. In the case of Judas, however, we see that there was no such thing. He did not have a new nature. He was not a true believer. In fact Christ had long before said, "Have I not chosen you twelve and one of you is a devil?" And so Judas did not return but went out and committed suicide.

John 6:70

What shall we say then about the multitude of people who have professed faith in Christ and have shown an interest in Christ and an interest in religion. There are some who will make a profession, for a while will soar to the heights and will become exceedingly enthusiastic and zealous in the things of Christ. But then, either suddenly or slowly, they will fall away; their zeal is no longer there; they are not concerned with the things of God; they go through the motions and finally even that ceases. Their hearts become cold.

What shall we say concerning these people? Well, we do not have to conjecture because the Bible teaches us very plainly about them. In the second chapter of the First Epistle of John, we are told this: "They went out from us, but they were not of us; for if they had been of us, they would no doubt have continued with us: but they went out, that they might be made manifest that they were not all of us."

1 John 2:19

Those who make professions do not necessarily possess what they profess. There are many hypocrites who outwardly may seem to profess an interest in the things of Christ but inwardly their hearts are unchanged. Finally their true colors are manifested and the true nature and desires of their hearts come forth and they turn to the world, the flesh, and the devil. The proverb is true that says the dog returns to his vomit and the sow that was washed unto the mire.

2 Peter 2:22

Now notice carefully the words from our text: "Whom he justified, *them* he also glorified." Justification is the first act of the Christian life; glorification is the first act in heaven. Justification is the first thing that happens to a Christian on earth. He is pardoned for his sins. He is accounted righteous in the sight of God. He is clothed with the righteousness of Jesus Christ. Glorification is the first thing that happens to the Christian in heaven. Every last vestige of sin is removed. He is made absolutely pure and holy, fit to stand in the presence of God. "Whom he

Romans 8:30

Romans 8:30

Romans 1:16

John 10:29

John 10:28

John 10:28

John 5:24

Romans 8:34

justified them he glorified." Those that begin the Christian life on earth end it in heaven. "For we are kept by the very power of God unto salvation," the Bible tells us.

Jesus said, "My Father, which gave them me, is greater than all; and no man is able to pluck them out of my Father's hand." I want to point out to you that there have been many efforts to try to circumvent the import of that passage. There are those who say that it could be the devil who could take them out. The Greek text simply says *no one*—it is not *man* but *no one*. There are others who have said, "Well, nobody can take us out, but we can take ourselves out." Are you not a man? Dare you say that you have the power to overcome the grasp of the Almighty God? No one can be taken out of His hand—that includes you. All of the forces of hell and earth cannot get them out of His hand. Do you suppose that you can get yourself out? Do you suppose that you would ever really want to?

Someone asked a Christian, "Are you not afraid that you will slip through His fingers!"

He replied, "Friend, I *am* one of His fingers!" Every true believer is part of the Body of Christ.

Now, if we have something for a few weeks, or months, or years, and then we lose it and die and go to hell, we may call that which we had whatever we want, but one thing that we can't call it is *eternal life*. At best it was a temporary blessing. But Jesus said, "I give unto them eternal life . . . ." Furthermore, He went on to say, "and they shall never perish . . . ." And should we receive eternal life and then perish, Christ is thus made a liar and God's Word is untrue. "I give unto them eternal life; and they shall never perish . . . ."

Jesus goes even further and says, "⌊They⌋ shall not come into condemnation." This is because we are not under the law but under grace. The law cannot condemn us because we are not under the law but we are under a covenant of grace. Therefore the law could do nothing. "Who is he that condemneth? It is Christ that died, yea . . . that is risen again." There is none to condemn us because Christ has taken for us our condemnation already.

There are others who say, "Well, why does God give us warnings in the Scripture against falling away if we cannot fall away?" If it is true, as Charles Spurgeon said, that we can fall many times on the deck of a ship, but God will not let us fall off the ship, then why are we warned against

apostasy? Why does the Bible say, "Take heed while ye
stand lest ye fall"? Why does the Scripture say, "I keep my
body under lest after I have preached to others I myself
should become a castaway"? One thing we need to note
here is that God is keeping us. But how is He keeping
us—by magic or by moral means?

1 Corinthians 10:12

1 Corinthians 9:27

Let me give you an example. I told my little daughter
Jennifer, who liked to get in the car when it was parked in
the driveway, not to ever fool with the gearshift because
that could release the gears and the car could roll down the
street and be hit by another car and she could be killed. I
severely warned her, "Never touch the gearshift." One
day, while out visiting, I was sitting in the living room and
saw her get into the car which was parked out front. She
couldn't see me, but I was watching her. All of a sudden I
saw the car make that little jerk it makes when it's just been
shifted out of park into neutral. I leaped out of my chair and
went flying out the door. I rushed to the car, pulled open
the door, and snatched Jennifer out—at which time I forth-
with gave her something which I hope will help to improve
her memory.

Now let us look at that incident. Why did I tell her not to
get into the car if I was going to rush out and stop it?
Because I want to train her to do what she ought to do. The
fact that I told her not to fool with the gearshift doesn't
mean that I wasn't going to do anything else.

There is a hymn that puts it well: "And, behind the dim
unknown, Standeth God within the shadow Keeping
watch above His own." God keeps us by moral means, not
by magic, and so we have these warnings which are repeated in the Scripture. Furthermore, we also know that by
our fall we can bring to ourselves grievous chastenings—as
my little girl is now aware; she didn't get killed but she did
get chastened.

This is Paul's conclusion of the whole doctrinal matter:
"For I am persuaded, that neither death, nor life, nor
angels, nor principalities, nor powers, nor things present,
nor things to come, Nor height, nor depth, nor any other
creature, shall be able to separate us from the love of God,
which is in Christ Jesus our Lord." And so it is in coming to
Christ. The Bible says, "Come unto me . . . whosoever
will ⌊may⌋ come . . . believe on the Lord Jesus Christ and
thou shalt be saved." It is as if it is all up to you and that's all
there is to it. But we know that, behind the shadows in the

Romans 8:38

Matthew 11:28

Mark 8:34
Acts 16:31

dim unknown, there is a Christ who says, "All that the Father giveth me shall come to me." None of those shall perish for this is the Father's will. There is a God who has said that He has loved us from before the foundation of the world; that we have been predestinated eternally to be conformed to the image of His Son.

And so it is with the keeping. Outwardly, God says in effect, "Keep yourself. If you walk off the road, you are going to get hurt! Stay on the road. Walk in the narrow way." But behind the shadows there is the One who says we are kept by the power of God unto salvation; there is the One who says that He is holding us with His almighty hand; there is the One who has said that He will never leave us or forsake us; there is the One who has said that the gifts and calling of God are not repented of; there is the One who has said that those whom He has justified He will also glorify.

We can take Him at His Word and rejoice not only that He has saved us but that He will keep us. We can say, "Yes, we believe in the perseverance of the saints." Consequently, you can say, "I *know* that I am on my way to Heaven!"

Father, we thank Thee that eternal life is a gift given and unrepented of. We thank Thee that we can become Thy saints, set aside and sanctified through simple faith in Jesus Christ; that even right now we can receive Him into our hearts as our Saviour and Lord. We can know that eternal life and salvation is all of grace; that it is all of God and not of man. Lord, we pray that Thou would save, that Thou would keep, that Thou would cause us to give ourselves wholly over to those means of our preservation: to the Word of God and to prayer, to service and obedience to Thee—lest we be deceived and supposing ourselves to be secured in carnal presumption, we should perish from the Way. In the name of Him who loves us and who gave Himself for us. *Amen.*

14 THE MOST UNPOPULAR SUBJECT IN THE WORLD

And whosoever was not found written in the book of life was cast into the lake of fire.

Revelation 20:15

After a long fatiguing day on a lecture trip to Pittsburgh, I flicked on the TV as I came into my hotel room. I was looking forward to a few moments of relaxation before turning in.

The program happened to be an interview talk show and, as my mind tuned to the discussion, I suddenly realized that over nationwide television the subject was wife and husband swapping.

The couple (husband and wife) being interviewed were obviously "swingers" and belonged to a group by the same name. After presenting views supporting their immoral life-style, the couple invited the audience to question them.

For the most part, the questions were pragmatic (wife and husband swapping didn't seem a practical way to run a marriage). But as each questioner presented an opposing view, the swingers demolished them with, "You're being too puritanical," or, "That's mid-Victorian!" And they weren't fazed by a weak question about how they thought God viewed their life-style.

Later, as I reflected on the program, it became apparent to me again that man will wax worse and worse when God is left out of his life. I was also reminded of Paul's statement in 1 Corinthians 5:1. What had been publicly aired on national TV was not even spoken of among the Gentiles! I realized afresh that all men need to understand that the Scriptures teach *there is a hell!*

I know many ranters, ravers, and demagogues have made the biblical doctrine of hell exceedingly distasteful. Some preachers have even spoken with apparent glee about the everlasting damnation of the wicked. I believe this to be truly sad. Because whenever anyone talks about hell and those who go there, he must understand they are real people with real flesh and real blood. Therefore, we must talk about hell with great sobriety and even tears, realizing it is what each of us deserves. Romans 3:10 says: ". . . There is none righteous, no, not one."

Yet most people outside of Christ dismiss the concept of hell. For them, the thought of endless and infinite misery so paralyzes their minds that they refuse to think about it. Others simply say, "I no longer believe in hell; it's too old-fashioned," which is like someone forming a society where all agree that Australia doesn't exist! But the reality of Australia would not change no matter how many people said it wasn't there. In the same way, God and His Word are not affected by whether men believe in Him or not. A majority never rules His Word out of court! The tragedy is there are millions of people in hell today, who, while on earth, closed their minds to its reality.

Frequently a person will tell me he believes in heaven but not hell. When I ask how they know there is a heaven, most say, "I haven't given the matter too much thought—I just feel there is."

Feelings of course are most unreliable. The only way any of us know about heaven is because God in His love tells us about it in His Word. The person who confesses he believes in heaven but not hell fails to realize that God reveals both in the Bible. The same Scriptures, that make known the glories and felicity of heaven, also make known the terrors and awfulness of hell. There is no logical consistency to accept heaven and deny hell.

1 Corinthians 5:1

Romans 3:10

Let us now, without being overwhelmed by our fears, take a rational and intelligent look at this matter. After repeatedly listening to a man punctuate his phraseology with *hell* one day, a friend of mine finally said, "Say, you seem to know a lot about hell. Is it because you've been there or because you're going there?"

Taken aback, the man said, "Well, I suppose I'm going there."

"You know," said my friend, "you don't have to."

That, of course, is what the Bible is saying to us: "You don't have to, you know!"

However, it's a psychological fact that men suppress the thing they fear most. I am convinced the person who fears hell most is the person who most vehemently denies its existence. But my word to you and the Word from Scripture is: No one need cringe in terror worrying about whether or not he will go to hell.

I once asked three people what they thought about hell before they became Christians. Their responses were identical. "I didn't like to think about it. But when I did, it was a most frightening prospect because I thought I might go there. I didn't know exactly what I had to do to get there, and I didn't know exactly what I had to do not to get there. I tried not to think about it."

I then asked what their thoughts and emotions were since their conversion. One said, "I am only afraid of it when I think of others. My fear is for them, not myself."

"Why are you now not afraid?" I asked. "Don't you believe it exists?"

"Yes," said all three. "We believe hell exists. But we're not afraid because we know we're not going there!"

This is an intelligent response to God's warning from Scripture. After warning us about hell, God doesn't leave us there. Rather He shows us a way of escape. God says that when a person by faith enters into a personal relationship with Jesus Christ, he is immediately saved from the penalty of hell. From that moment on throughout the rest of his life and into eternity, he has the assurance from Scripture that he shall never see hell.

John 3:18

If a person has never entered into a personal relationship with Jesus Christ (even though he may have been a church member for years), then such a person has reason to fear hell.

Let me repeat! The person who refuses to believe in hell, or who thinks that denying its existence will make it go away, is deceiving himself. Jesus Christ Himself more than any other person in Scripture talks about the awful reality of hell. But when Jesus spoke about hell, He didn't speak to frighten. Rather He spoke to warn and offer Himself as the alternative to hell.

Sometimes people ask if the Scriptures talk about hell as an actual place. Indeed the Bible does. Look at some of the descriptive terms used:

Matthew 25:41   . . . everlasting fire, prepared for the devil and his angels . . . .

     . . . hell fire: Where the worm dieth not, and the fire is not quenched . . . .

Mark 9:47, 48

Revelation 21:8   . . . the lake which burneth with fire and brimstone . . . .

Revelation 9:1, 2   . . . the bottomless pit . . . .

Matthew 8:12   . . . outer darkness . . . .

Matthew 13:42   . . . [a place where there is] wailing and gnashing of teeth.

Luke 16:24   It's a place where one cries, ". . . I am tormented in this flame." It's a place where "the smoke of their torment ascendeth up for *ever and ever:* and they have no rest day

Revelation 14:11   nor night."

In each case, all the Greek words used mean *everlasting, unending, eternal.* They are the strongest words found in Greek for *never-ending duration.*

The great A. A. Hodge said that all the great church fathers, Reformers, and biblical scholars, with all of their dictionaries, lexicons (both Hebrew and Greek), commentaries, and systematic theologies, concur that the Scriptures teach an endless punishment of the finally impenitent, and this in spite of a tremendous human desire in the opposite direction. So state all the creeds of the Presbyterians, Episcopalians, Lutherans, Methodists, Congregationalists, Roman Catholics, Greek Orthodox, and all the historic churches of Protestantism. Indeed it is a mistaken philanthropy that would give any encouragement of escaping the biblical injunction of impending doom to those who die outside of Christ. It is a mock charity which would encourage the impenitent to suppose that there is any chance that God does not mean what He says.

There are those who try to create a divinity from their own minds and inflate it with their own conjectures. At best, their god becomes a wishy-washy idol without holiness, justice, or righteousness.

Those who suppose that God is too loving to ever punish sin do not know the God who has revealed Himself in Scripture. Those who also suppose man is too good for such a fate do not know the revelation of the heart of man which is revealed to us in the Bible. But those who realize God is holy—that man is depraved, his heart unclean—realize their hope lies in the death and Resurrection of Jesus Christ. Because, on a cross outside the city wall of Jerusalem, the Son of God endured the wrath of His Father for those that would trust in Him.

I am convinced the only way anyone will come to appreciate the biblical teachings on hell is to know in his heart that he will never see it. Our Lord said, "There is a broad way which leadeth to destruction, and a narrow way which leadeth unto life." There is a Book of Life and those whose names are in it shall go into everlasting bliss. Those whose names are not found written in the Book of Life shall be cast into the lake of fire. God has set His seal to it. His Word is true.

Matthew 7:13, 14

Revelation 20:15

Is your name in that book? Are you on that narrow way which leads to life? Do you want to know God's way of escape? Our hope is simply this: Christ died on a cross and we who trust in Him may by His grace go to heaven.

Have you by faith laid hold of Jesus Christ and invited Him into your heart? Have you repented of your sins? The promise of God is: ". . . Whosoever was not found written in the book of life was cast into the lake of fire."

Revelation 20:15

For those of you who have never personally accepted Jesus Christ into your life and want to, why don't you pray these simple words:

"Heavenly Father, this day I embrace Your Son, Jesus Christ, as my personal Saviour. I take into my own heart the One who came that I might live. Therefore by faith I claim and believe the promise that he that trusteth in You shall not come into condemnation but is passed from death unto life. I rejoice that by Your grace I shall never see the bottomless pit and outer darkness. I thank You, Father, because now that I have taken Christ as my Saviour, I shall in the moment of death be transported into paradise to be with You forever and ever." *Amen.*

John 5:24

Father, the great purity of Your holiness stands in stark contrast to our sin. In our heart of hearts, we know none of us is righteous. O God, may we this day behold the Lamb of God, which taketh away the sin of the world. Help us to know the only way of escape

John 1:29

is through a personal response to God's love in providing His Son, Jesus Christ, to die on the cross for the punishment we condignly deserve.

Father, if there are those whose hearts are still not right with You, I pray the Holy Spirit will incline them to repent and turn to Jesus who stands with hands outstretched. *Amen.*

15 THE LIFE HEREAFTER: HEAVEN

In my Father's house are many mansions: if it were not so, I would have told you. I go to prepare a place for you. And if I go and prepare a place for you, I will come again, and receive you unto myself; that where I am, there ye may be also.

John 14:2, 3

God has created us for eternity. Yet most of us act as if He had created us merely for this life. In centuries gone by, it used to be said of some people that they were "too otherworldly"—too heavenly minded. This is certainly not something that can be said about very many people today, for we live in a time which is so this-worldly, when people have all of their attention fixed on the world, the flesh, and the devil. The result is a society that is falling apart as everybody rushes to get more of that which satisfies the flesh. The people are like those whom Paul described when he said, "Whose end is destruction, whose God is their belly . . . ."

Philippians 3:19

I believe that a healthy antidote to the cancer that is eating away at our society today would be a little healthful otherworldliness. If heaven is our home, if heaven is our destination, if heaven is the greatest thing that man can ever contemplate, how much time do you spend in thinking about it? It might be an indicator of whether or not you are going there—because those that are have a foretaste, an earnest, in their hearts now; and those that are not probably never give it a thought.

Heaven! What is it? Well, it's a major theme of the Scriptures. It's mentioned five hundred fifty times in the Bible by that name alone. It is also called by many other names. It is the better country which the prophets sought after. It is called not only a country but also a city. ". . . a city which hath foundations, whose builder and maker is God." It is also called a house. "In my Father's house are many mansions." Furthermore, it is a real locality. Jesus said, "I go to prepare a place for you. . . ."

Concerning the passage of Scripture we have before us, there have been those who have talked about the heavenly city of Jerusalem and have said, "My, if that were actually a picture of heaven, we'd be so jammed up together that we wouldn't have space to turn around! Just imagine all of the people of heaven in one little city!" There have often been those who have scoffed at the Word of God; their problem has been that they have never really examined it carefully. In Revelation 21:16, we read of the city which lieth four square; a city which was measured at 12 thousand furlongs long and 12 thousand furlongs wide. Now a furlong is an eighth of a mile which means that this is a city which is 15 hundred miles long and 15 hundred miles wide; or a city as long as from Florida to Maine and from New York to the Mississippi River. That's a pretty good sized city! That would be a megalopolis of the first order.

Imagine what this city would be like because it is not only 12 thousand furlongs wide and long, but it is also 12 thousand furlongs high, according to this passage—for its height and length and breadth are equal. The Empire State building has just over one hundred stories. This is a city that if it had stories—not of merely nine or ten feet in height but a commodious fifteen feet in height—would have 528 thousand stories! And on each of these stories there would be 2250 thousand square—not feet!—but miles!—for a grand total in all of this heavenly city of 1 trillion, 188 billion square miles!

Now the department of eugenics has estimated that since man first began on this planet until today, there have lived approximately 30 billion people. One mathematician did a little figuring and came up with the fact that this would

Hebrews 11:10

John 14:2

Revelation 21:16

mean there would be 198 square miles for each family in this Holy City—*if* everybody who ever lived went there! And Jesus said, "Few there be that find the way and many there are which go into destruction." If even half the people made it, there would still be about four hundred square miles per family—a very good size piece of real estate as anyone can attest. I think that ought to be enough space for you to turn around! I wouldn't want to press that place which "eye hath not seen, nor ear heard, neither have entered into the heart of man [what] God hath prepared for [us]," into any straightjacket of human words. I am sure that all of these descriptions are merely symbols which stir up our imagination but cannot begin to describe the beauties of that better country which God has prepared for us.

Heaven! Do you think about it very much? "Where will it be?" is a question which some people ask. Let me say this: Heaven is a real place, for Jesus said, "I go to prepare a place for you." The Greek word for place is *topos* from which we get *topography*—the study of places. It is not a state of mind, nor is it here on this earth now, for some people say we have our heaven or hell now. But Jesus said, "And as it is appointed unto men once to die, but after this the judgment"—and then comes heaven or hell. It is after this life. Where is it? Now any high-school astronomer will tell you that, if you look up into the sidereal heavens, you will find they are everywhere filled with sparkling galaxies, except in one place. Directly overhead to the north there is a great vast blackness which the most powerful of our telescopes have not been able to penetrate.

Of course we know that there was a Russian cosmonaut who went into space and when he came back he assured us that there was neither a God nor a heaven. Recently he took a far longer trip, and when they lowered his body into the grave many Russians cast fir branches in after him (the fir branch is a Russian symbol of immortality). Atheists? May I point out that Kosygin cast one also. The cosmonaut knows better now. But just think! He had gone up and taken a look and it wasn't there! But where did he look? Imagine the billions of galaxies the size of our Milky Way (which has billions of suns in itself) and in this one small galaxy known as the Milky Way (millions of galaxies are far larger) there is a third-rate little star called *sun*, and that sun is invisible from much of our own galaxy. Around that little

Matthew 7:13, 14

1 Corinthians 2:9

John 14:2

Hebrews 9:27

tiny sun there rotate nine planets, all of which are invisible from our nearest neighboring star. Around one of the smaller of those planets there circles a moon, so close as to be indistinguishable from other planets in our own solar system. Somewhere between the moon and our earth, and so far closer to our earth as to be practically crawling on its surface, there went out a little Russian cosmonaut to examine the cosmos! And he found that God was not there! This reminds me of the little child, sailing his little boat around his bathtub, coming to the conclusion that Africa really isn't there because it's not at this end of the bathtub and it's not at that end of the bathtub!

Revelation 21:2

John said he saw the Holy City descending out of heaven as a bride adorned for her husband. The great Dr. Charles Hodge of Princeton, the orthodox of the orthodox, has stated that it has been the consensus of orthodox theologians that the final abode of the redeemed after the judgment will be not only in heaven but also on the new earth. John says there will be a new heaven and a new earth. This earth will be purged by fire, reconstituted, glorified, and it seems that the dwelling place of the redeemed will be throughout the entire universe which will be delivered from the bondage of sin at that time. How great will be the intellectual stimulation of inhabitating a sinless universe which is now beyond our very comprehension in its magnitude.

Revelation 21:1

What will it be like? First of all, we will not be there as any Casper-the-ghost type sitting on a cloud playing a harp. Occasionally, I talk to people who say they are not interested in going to heaven. When I hear a statement like that, I can either conclude (1) that this person does not believe there is a heaven, or (2) they are so intolerably ignorant, so sluggish of mind and intellect, that it would be amazing if they could be interested in anything more than their own navels! Because, if there's anything in this world that is deserving of human interest, it is the greatest thing which ever man has conceived of: the very paradise of God. If a person should be wholly taken up and his interest consumed with the pathetic things which are twisted and distorted with sin, how infinitely more interesting will be the new heaven and the new earth.

We will have glorified bodies. Our senses will be enlarged greatly in their capacities. Already we know, that compared to some of the other creatures in this world, we are almost blind, deaf, and dumb. What will it be like then when we are released from the bondage of sin? If we can hear beautiful music now which causes our hearts to thrill, when we are limited to a tiny, narrow wedge of the spectrum of sound, what will it be like when our ears are opened that we may hear all of the vast harmonies of heaven? Right now we are almost blind when compared to the telescopic and microscopic sight of some birds. We can hardly see at all, and yet what will it be like when our vision is such as it will be in perfected bodies?

Beyond that there is the infinite continuous progress of knowledge. Moral perfection does not do away with progress. There is such a thing as progress in perfection. Adam was perfect yet he was not omniscient. He did not know all things; and he grew in knowledge. Jesus was perfect and yet the Bible says He also grew in wisdom and in knowledge. So, also, we who now know in part shall then know in full. How wonderful it will be to begin to use some of the capacity of the human mind which in the state of sin remains about 90 percent unused—even by the greatest genius that has ever lived. What a tremendous intellectual adventure it will be!

Then, of course, there will be the exemption from all sorrow. As Dr. Charles Hodge tells us, "What is it that takes away the joy of this life? Whatever it is it will be gone then." For many people it will be pain. It comes and disturbs their sleep. It knocks upon the door uninvited and unwelcomed as an intruder. It slips into the very crevices of their bones. It throbs and beats and aches. How many there are who, if they could only be delivered from pain, would feel that they had entered into paradise already. But there will be no more pain there. "Neither sorrow," the Bible says. That pain of soul. How many people have had the very joy of life sucked out of them by the sorrow of loss of a loved one. Their hearts have been deflated and it seems as if life will never have joy again. There will be no more sorrow then, nor will there be any more death, for there will be the continued enjoyment of all the blessings of heaven.

Also there will be no more sin. We don't realize that sin is what really takes away the joy of living. What a blessed fellowship—what a blessed communion there will be with the saints when there is no more sin, no more selfishness, no more anger or temper, no more pride or deceit, no more walking in darkness covering up the real intent of the heart.

Revelation 21:4

But there will be pure and perfect love. What a communion of souls and hearts as they are outpoured to one another in the great adventures that stretch before us forever in heaven.

— Of course there will also be the outward and external beauties of that place. I was in Oregon and how magnificent is that country with its beautiful mountains jutting into the sky. If this world under the burden of sin can show us something of beauty, what is this but crumbs off the table compared to that indescribable beauty that will exist in the very paradise of the Infinite God.

There will be the security that it shall never be lost. Whatever you have in this life and wherever you dwell, in South Florida with all of its loveliness, or in the Swiss Alps, or wherever you might be, if you have all the wealth that man could want and the most beautiful of possessions, you will know that one day all of these are going to slip from your grasp. There is that dread of loss that old age brings when so many people live in constant anxiety concerning their loss of all things. There will be here eternal security —the continued and never-ending enjoyment of all good forever. This will be the blessing of heaven.

There will be a blessing of reunion there also. I remember a touching story concerning Tony Fontaine whose beautiful voice has lifted the hearts of many. His mother and father were devout Christians who worked in poverty-stricken areas for Christ. But their own child rebelled and wanted nothing to do with their disciplined life and their love for Christ. He was going to sow his wild oats and seek fame and fortune in this world with the talent that God had given him, but which he seemed to think was of his own making. He set out for Hollywood and became famous, and all the time his mother prayed for him. Night after night she would anoint her pillow with tears for her boy Tony. She grew old and sick and Tony still did not come to Christ. Finally she died and left her son still unsaved.

Sometime later Tony was again confronted with the gospel. By the providence of God, he was brought to the cross and he embraced the Saviour as his own. He committed his life, his soul, his talent, and his all to Christ, and has since used his voice to change many a life.

One day while he was singing out on the West Coast, a woman came up to him (he had told his life story and had mentioned his mother) and said, "I'm leaving this week and I'd be glad to carry a message to your mother if you'd like."

He said, "I—I thank you, but you didn't understand me. My mother is dead."

This elderly woman said, "Oh, yes, I understood you perfectly. But you see, I'm going where she is and I'd be glad to carry a message to her if you'd like."

He stopped and thought, and said those words which he has sung so often: "Tell my mother I'll be there, in answer to her prayer. Tell my mother, tell my mother, I'll be there." Sometime later he learned that this lady died that very week, and I'm sure that the message was delivered.

What a blessed time of reunion that will be. One man said he really never understood what Jesus meant by treasure in heaven until he had lost a child. When that treasure had been deposited in heaven, he said, "Ah, my heart is there now. How real heaven became for me." For where your treasure is, there your heart will be also. How blessed will be the reunions in heaven on that day. It is a place where there will be no more "good-byes"—only "hellos."

Matthew 6:21

The real question is not, has a place been prepared for us, but are we prepared for that place? Will your name be called? Will your name be found written there?

The battlefield was strewn with bodies. The surgeon had done his best, and now he sat down for a moment of rest. Suddenly one cried out, "Here!"

The surgeon leaped up and ran to him and knelt at his side and said, "Yes, son, what can I do for you?"

The soldier opened his eyes, surprised, and said, "Nothing. They're calling the roll in heaven. They just called my name and I answered."

Will your name be found in the Lamb's Book of Life? You can have heaven there only by having it here. Life eternal is in Jesus Christ and those who have received Jesus Christ here are those who will enter into life there. Christ said, "I am the way . . . no man cometh unto the Father but by me." Christ is life—life abundant and life eternal and those who receive Him into their hearts as Lord and King and Saviour and Master, are the ones that are going to be there. Will you be among them? Have you received the King of Heaven as the King of your heart?

John 14:6

If you are going to heaven, there is one way that you can tell: *You know it.* "For these things are written that you may *know* that you have eternal life," the Scripture says. If you

1 John 5:13

don't know that you are going to heaven, my friend, you're not—because if you are, you know it. God does not give His greatest gift without giving some assurance of its possession. Have you received Christ? Is He your All in all? Is He the One in whom you trust alone or are you still resting on the poor and pitiful rags of your own righteousness? Can you sing, "Blessed assurance, Jesus is mine! Oh, what a foretaste of glory divine!"?

I am going to heaven. This I know. I do not deserve it, I never have, and I never will. But by the pure unmerited grace of God, through the cross of Jesus Christ my Saviour, I am going to paradise forever—and ever—and ever—and ever. *Are you?*

O Lord, for those who yet walk in darkness, staggering through the blackness of this world on their way to an eternal death, may the light of life shine upon their hearts; may they see their sin and their hopelessness. May they look into the face of Christ upon the cross and know that for this cause came He from heaven; for this cause laid He aside His glory, became incarnate in human flesh. For us and for our sin, He died that the penalty might be paid —that the gift of God might be given which is life eternal. Lord, may they this hour believe. May their hearts this hour cry out, "Lord Jesus, I open the door. Come, Thou who art light and life and peace and joy. Come and bring with Thee Thy heaven. Dwell in my heart by faith. I receive Thee. I trust Thee. I commit myself unto Thee. Take me and make me Thine own, that I may love Thee now and love Thee forevermore." In Thy lovely name. *Amen and Amen.*

16 THE BIBLE

In the beginning was the Word, and the Word was with God, and the Word was God.

John 1:1

Our Lord Jesus Christ said, "Sanctify [change or transform] them through thy truth: thy word is truth." We are changed, our lives are transformed by the truth of God. The truth of God is living, vital, and life-transforming and it is vitally important, especially in this day of confusion, this day of ignorance concerning the things of God, that Christian people be well established concerning the truth of God's Word.

John 17:17

I talked with a young lady recently and, after ascertaining that she believed the Bible to be the Word of God, I said to her, "Tell me, what would you say to people who asked you to prove that the Bible is the Word of God? What would you tell them?"

She thought about that for a little while and said, "I wouldn't know what to say to them."

You say that you believe that the Bible is the Word of God. Is this simply some blind belief, some leap into darkness, some wish being the father to the thought; or is there any substantive proof, any demonstration of the fact that the Bible is, indeed, the Word of God? I wonder how many of you would know what to tell a person if he said, "Show me why you believe that this Book is inspired by God. There are many books that claim to be inspired; there are many books that have been taken to be inspired revelations. How do you know which one is the truth?"

I was told that a recent book entitled *Dust of Death* by Os Guinness pointed out that the great intrusion of oriental religions into America in recent times is because people do not have a grasp of the meaning of divine revelation. They do not understand what the Bible teaches about the nature, the uniqueness, the once-for-allness of the revelation that God has given to us in the Scripture. Therefore, they go after any sort of experiential or mystic type of experience that they think is going to give them some contact with God.

How do you know that the Bible is the Word of God? That is a good question to face when we are approaching any branch of human learning. It is what is known as the *epistemological question*. Epistemology is the study of how you know something. It is the science of knowledge. How do you know? That is the epistemological question. How do you know the Bible is the Word of God? How do you know that a prophet is sent from God? The Bible answers those questions very clearly.

Let us examine the matter. We note that the Bible explicitly and repeatedly *claims* to be the Word of God. It claims to be a revelation from God Almighty to mankind. Now that may not seem strange or even relevant to some, but I would point out that many of the scriptures of various great religions make no such claim at all. There is not the slightest hint in the writings of Confucius that they are a divine revelation. He never dreamed of them as being such. Nor does Buddha claim for his writings any sort of divine revelation. So we see that in many of the great religions of the world no such claim is made; but over two thousand times in the Old Testament alone, the claim is made: "Thus saith the Lord . . . then the word of the Lord came unto Jeremiah the prophet . . . ." Over and over again, "Thus saith the Lord." The *claim* is made.

Jeremiah 28:12

Now I will readily grant to anyone that making a claim and substantiating it are two entirely different matters. But if the claim were not even made then some would no doubt say, "The Christians are claiming for the Bible that which it never claims for itself, namely, to be a revelation from God." Even as you may have heard somebody say it some-

time, "Well, Jesus never claimed to be the Messiah." Have
you ever heard that? Well that is part of the invincible
ignorance that prevails in this country today concerning
the Scriptures. Even the most cursory reading of the Gos-
pels would convince someone that that is not the case.

In the third chapter of John, the woman at the well says to
Christ, "I know that Messias cometh, . . . he will tell us
all things." Jesus replied, "I that speak unto thee am he."
How much more explicit a claim could you want? He repeated it several more times and, lastly, under oath before
the Sanhedrin when He was asked if He were the Christ the
Son of the living God, He replied, "I am." Well, so also the
Scriptures claim to be the Word of God. If the Scriptures
didn't make it, then some people would say that we were
trying to claim for Scripture something that it did not claim
for itself.

John 4:25
John 4:26

Matthew 26:63, 64

But then, are we going to demonstrate that this claim is
true? The same people who would be likely to make a
statement like that are the people who will say, "Well, the
Bible is full of contradictions and errors." I'm sure you have
heard that many times. I would suggest a simple reply
which I have used many times. I simply pull the New
Testament out of my coat pocket and say to them, "That is
very interesting. I've been studying the Bible for years and I
haven't been able to find one. Would you be so kind as to
show me where they are?" I'm still waiting to be shown.
No, the Bible is not full of contradictions and errors and the
people that most facilely make the claim are usually those
that know least about what the Bible teaches. Usually they
are people who have never even read it once. We might
remind them that, for example, A. T. Robertson, whose
massive work entitled *Greek Grammar In Light of Historical
Research* is the greatest work on Greek grammar that has
ever been written, believed in the absolute infallibility of
the Scriptures. Dr. Robert Dick Wilson of Princeton, probably the greatest linguist who ever lived and who knew
forty-six different languages, believed that the Old Testament was absolutely trustworthy. W. F. Arndt and F. W.
Gingrich, authors of the most modern Greek lexicon that
we have today in which every word in the Greek Testament
is examined from virtually all of ancient Greek literature,
provide the most microscopic examination of the full meaning of all of the words in the entire Greek New Testament.
Yet these scholars believe absolutely that the Bible is infal-

libly true and without contradiction in the least. W. F. Arndt even has a book entitled *Does the Bible Contradict Itself?* in which he takes several of the supposed contradictions mustered by those who have been placed on the spot, and shows that they are only of the most superficial type. Even the most cursory examination beneath the surface shows them to be no contradictions at all. No, the Bible is not full of contradictions and errors but is, indeed, the very Word of God.

Deuteronomy 18:22

How can we prove it? God tells us very plainly how we can prove it. How will you know that a prophet is sent from God? God presents us with that same question: "How will you know that a prophet is sent from me? By this ye shall know, that he shall tell the future and if what he prophesies does not come to pass then I have not sent him." The gift of prophecy is one of the methods by which the Bible authenticates itself as the Word of God. Now, some people would again not appreciate the significance of this because they do not realize that this also is something which is strikingly absent from all other religious writings. For example, the writings of Buddha are totally lacking in any sort of specific predictive prophecy about the things of the future. In the writings of Confucius, there is absolutely no hint of any predictive prophecies. In the case of the Koran, the scriptures of the Muslims, we find only the prophecy of Mohammed that he would return to Mecca, "self-fulfilling prophecy," which he himself of course fulfilled. This is quite different from the prophecy of Christ, who said that He would rise from the dead. And that is just one of several thousands of prophecies that occur in the Scriptures and which are of the most specific, concrete, and definite nature.

1 Thessalonians 5:20, 21

The Bible says, "Despise not prophesying. Prove all things; hold fast that which is good." Some people will say, "Oh, well, these prophecies were just vague and general prophecies such as the prophecy of the Delphian Oracle, who prophesied that when two Roman generals met outside the City of Rome to fight a war, the enemy of Rome would be destroyed. Well, both of them took heart in that prophecy, supposing themselves to be the friend of Rome. Obviously that prophecy could not help but be fulfilled one way or the other." Or the skeptics might say, "Well, we have people who prophesy today." Do we? Is that true? Let us take a look. Probably the most notable is Jeane Dixon.

Here is a prophet who we are told has made amazing prophecies with astounding accuracy—but we are not told about all of the mistakes! Take the decade of the fifties, for example. She prophesied all of the candidates of each of the major political parties, and she prophesied the winner of each of three presidential elections, fifty-two, fifty-six, and sixty. How well did she do? Well, by flipping a coin you could have done reasonably well—but her record for that whole decade was zero! She missed every candidate in every party and every winner of every presidential election. That you probably haven't heard before. And so we see that there is a vast jump that separates the prophecies of someone like this from the unfailing prophecies of the Scripture, which have all come to pass as they were supposed to.

Let us take a closer look at them. We see that these prophecies concern many subjects, including two that I would like to look at more thoroughly. We could take the time to examine the life of Christ. There are three hundred and thirty-three specific prophecies concerning the life of Christ in the Old Testament, but I assume they are fairly well known.

I would, however, like to look at the fact that almost every major city, and virtually every nation, within a thousand miles of Israel had its entire future prophesied by the Bible. So these are prophecies so specific, so concrete, so definite that anybody can tell whether or not they have been fulfilled. Any high-school student with an encyclopedia could check up on them, yet most people simply ignore them or are not even aware of the fact that they exist.

First of all, look at the prophecies concerning the cities of Tyre and Sidon. You might note that the prophecies concerning both cities and nations are of very different types. Some prophecies say that the cities and nations will be entirely eradicated. They will be destroyed and they will never again be inhabited. Other cities are to be decimated, put to the sword, but they will continue. Others will be diminished, made base, but they will exist down through the centuries. This is amazing! Suppose that these prophecies were reversed. How the skeptics would rejoice with glee! Yet they are unfailingly, infallibly accurate. For example, with Tyre and Sidon: Tyre was the capital of the world for two thousand years and it had grown until it had become to the sea what Babylon was to the land. Carthage

Isaiah 23:15

Ezekiel 26:4, 5, 12, 14

Ezekiel 26:7

was but one of the colonies of Tyre when Ezekiel uttered his famous prophecies about this great city. He said this (and notice the specific nature of the prophecy), "And they shall destroy the walls of Tyrus, and break down her towers: I will also scrape her dust from her, and make her like the top of a rock. It shall be a place for the spreading of nets in the midst of the sea: for I have spoken it, saith the Lord God. . . . they shall lay thy stones and thy timber and thy dust in the midst of the water. And I will make thee like the top of a rock. Thou shalt be built no more: for I the Lord have spoken it." Well, what happened? Some years after Ezekiel made his prophecy, Nebuchadnezzar, the mighty monarch of Babylon, invaded the coastal regions and besieged the city of Tyre. For thirteen years, he laid siege to the mighty walls of the city of Tyre and finally breached them. The horses of Nebuchadnezzar rode into the streets of Tyre, the population was put to the sword, and blood flowed like wine. The city was sacked, a few of the towers were destroyed, a few holes were made in the walls, the city was burned, and Nebuchadnezzar returned to Babylon. Was the prophecy fulfilled? Only in a small part. The city was destroyed, but there, jutting up into the horizon over the bleak Mediterranean, could be seen the remains of the walls and the mighty towers of Tyre. There within those walls great piles of huge stones, timbers, and dust bore eloquent testimony to the fact that prophecies were not fulfilled. Yet God had spoken specifically of these things. Who now would ever do what He had prophesied? Who would come and level the walls of this city? Who would come and take the huge stones of this city and dump them in the sea? Who would take the timbers and throw them in the ocean and even scrape the dust until this great mound of rubble would become like a bare rock, a place for the spreading of nets? What mad man would do these things? Who would guarantee that this city would be built and inhabited no more?

Note also that Ezekiel did not prophesy after the event for he died, and another century went by, and another, and another half a century. A quarter of a millennium later the city still stood there as mute testimony to the fact that the prophecy had not yet been completely fulfilled! And then, like a bugle call, there came a thrill of terror out of the north—as a mighty conqueror appeared on the horizon. Clad in silver with armor of gold, plumed helmet, and

astride his mighty white horse Bucephalus—there came
that mighty one, followed by the massive phalanxes of
Greece, whose name was Alexander the Great—a name
which sent shivers of fear down the spines of those of
Persia. There at the Issus he met the mighty monarch of
Persia and dealt him his first crushing blow. The king fled
to the south and then to the east. Before Alexander followed
him inland, however, he decided to nullify the force of the
great Persian navy by sealing off all of its seaports. One by
one they surrendered but then he came to Tyre, half a mile
out in the Mediterranean Sea, built on an island. How
could he get at it? He demanded they surrender. They
laughed at him. They were impregnable in their ocean
fortress. Finally, Alexander conceived one of the most dar-
ing and most brilliant schemes in the history of warfare. He
would build a causeway across the half a mile of the
Mediterranean Sea and he would utterly destroy this city
that had thwarted his plans. Where would they find the
material? "Tear down the towers! Destroy the walls! Take
the huge stones and the timbers and cast them into the
sea!"

Some years ago I picked up a little book entitled *Alexander the Great* by Charles Mercer, with consultant Cornelius
C. Vermeule III, the Curator of Classical Art at the Museum
of Fine Arts in Boston. This book includes a most amazing
description: "Mainland Tyre was leveled, and its rubble
was carried to the construction site. Meanwhile, logs were
dragged from the forests of Lebanon, and quarries were
opened in the hills to supply stones for Diades' fabulous
highway . . . Alexander himself carried stones on his
back. "Rubble, logs, stones!" They shall lay [Tyre's] stones
and thy timber and thy dust in the midst of the water." Two
and a half centuries after that prophecy it was fulfilled!

Ezekiel 26:12

Yet still the prophecy was not *completely* fulfilled, for yet
more was to be done to the city of Tyre. It had been scraped
clean and now was like a rock. It was to become a "place to
spread nets upon." Constantin Volney, the great skeptic,
told of seeing fishermen spread their nets there. I, myself,
have seen pictures showing the nets of fishermen spread on
the rock of Tyre.

Ezekiel 26:14

Now compare the prophecies concerning Sidon, a few
miles to the north. God said that famine and pestilence
would come there and He would send the sword, but the
city would continue. And so it did! It was never completely

Isaiah 23
Jeremiah 27:3–6; 47:4
Ezekiel 28:23

destroyed, although it was sacked and pillaged many times. It continued, despite this plunder, to exist down to our day. Suppose the prophet had gotten his prophecies mixed up!

Take another pair of cities of similar type: Samaria and Jerusalem, the capital of the kingdom of the south and the capital of the kingdom of the north. Concerning Jerusalem, it is well known God stated that He would destroy this city by Nebuchadnezzer—He would tear down its mighty walls. But He also said that the walls would be built again, in troublous times. The walls would be built and the city would be reinhabited. Of course we all know that is true. I have stood on top of those mighty walls and walked atop part of their length. They are there today, an awesome sight; but what about the great walls of the mighty city of Samaria, built high upon a mountain? Of those walls God said that He would cast down the rocks into the valley below, that He would destroy the city, that He would make it into a vineyard, and that He would uncover the foundations of that city. I have visited the city of Samaria, and what did I see? Without even being aware of these particular prophecies, I remember looking over the cliff down thousands of feet below to see the huge boulders that had once been the walls of Samaria. I remember having the various trees and plantings (olive trees and the vineyards) pointed out to us by the guide. Then I saw the great depths of excavations where all of the walls of other centuries, one dynasty after another, had been exposed. The very foundations of Samaria were laid bare! These are but a few of the prophecies concerning cities.

We know that God says concerning cities like Ashdod (which I have also visited) "and I will cut off the inhabitant from Ashdod." Complete and crystal clear definition of the fact that this city is going to be completely destroyed! There is absolutely nothing living there—it is complete and total desolation. There is not the first house or shack or tent where once Ashdod was.

The same is true of Ashkelon. "Ashkelon shall be a desolation. It shall not be inhabited." Today, almost twenty-five hundred years later, Ashkelon is still uninhabited and still a desolation! This is attested by Constantin Volney who refers to "the deserted ruins of Azkalan" (*Volney's Travels*, vol. 2, p. 338).

If you feel that those interpretations are subjective, let me

Jeremiah 24:9; 29:21; 35:17

Isaiah 4:3–6

Micah 1:5, 6

Amos 1:8

Zephaniah 2:4
Zechariah 9:5

point out to you that I am using as reference the writings of
various skeptics garnered from the collection of Dr. Alexander Keith. Skeptics quoted are such men as Constantin
Volney, who made Abraham Lincoln into a skeptic for most
of his earlier years, and Edward Gibbon, the author of *The
Rise and Fall of the Roman Empire,* who was a notorious
skeptic.

All of the cities of Edom were to be destroyed. The   Jeremiah 49:17
prophecies are very striking and very specific. Jeremiah
says, "And Edom (or Idumea) shall be a
desolation . . . . As in the overthrow of Sodom and
Gomorrah and the neighbor cities thereof, saith the Lord,
no man shall abide there, neither shall a son of man dwell in
it." Ezekiel is even more emphatic. He declares that be-   Jeremiah 49:17, 18
cause Edom, or Mount Seir (the Mount of Edom), had
fought against the Israelites in the time of their calamity,
God will utterly destroy them. He says, "Thus saith the
Lord God; Behold, O Mount Seir, I am against thee, and I
will stretch out mine hand against thee, and I will make
thee most desolate. I will lay thy cities waste, and thou shalt   Ezekiel 35:3, 4
be desolate, and thou shalt know that I am the Lord. I will
make thee perpetual desolations, and *thy cities shall not
return:* and *ye shall know that I am the Lord.*" Ezekiel further   Ezekiel 35:9
describes the extent of the desolation which shall fall upon
the land of Edom, "I will also stretch out mine hand upon
Edom, and . . . will make it desolate from Teman."   Ezekiel 25:13

These are startling prophecies. They are exceedingly
specific. No one is to live in these cities; no son is to be born
in them; and the cities shall not return. Thus we will know
that the Lord is God. The extent of the desolation both
geographically and chronologically is described. Here is a
bold gauntlet thrown down before unbelievers. Have these
spectacular prophecies come to pass? Listen to the writings
of various skeptics and other travelers in the Near East.
Concerning Edom, Constantin Volney says that the traces
of many towns and villages are met with. At present *all this
country* is a desert. Also concerning Edom, John L. Burckhardt declares, "And Maan is *the only inhabited place in it*"
(*Burckhardt's Travels,* p. 436). Even the nature of the desolation is described by Jeremiah. "If grapegatherers come to
thee, would they not leave some gleaning grapes? If thieves
by night, they will destroy till they have enough. But I have
made Esau [Edom] bare." Burckhardt declares that the   Jeremiah 49:9, 10
whole plain presented to the view an expanse of shifting

sands, the depth of sand precludes all vegetation of herbage" (*Burckhardt's Travels in Syria,* p. 442). According to the prophet, cities of Mount Edom, or Mount Seir, were to be ruined and laid waste. According to Burckhardt "The following ruined places are situated in Mount Seir, Kalaab, Djirba, Eyl, Ferdakh, Anyk, Birel-Beytar, Shemakh, and Syk" (*Burckhardt's Travels in Syria,* pp. 443, 444). Commenting on the statement that by this desolation, "ye shall know that I am the Lord," Stephen, a Christian standing among the ruins of Petra, the capital of Edom, declares, "I would that the skeptic could stand as I did among the ruins of this city, among the rocks, and there open the Sacred Book, and read the words of the inspired penmen, written when this desolate place was one of the greatest cities in the world. I see the scoff arrested, his cheek pale, his lip quivering, and his heart quaking with fear, as the ruined city cries out to him in a voice loud and powerful as that of one risen from the dead. Though he would not believe Moses and the prophets, he believes the handwriting of God Himself and the desolation and eternal ruin around him" (*Stephen's Incidents of Travel in Arabia. Petraea*).

Ezekiel 6:7

Let us now look at some of the even larger examples of the prophecies of God concerning whole nations and their capital cities. Examine the city of Nineveh, the capital of the great Assyrian Empire. Nineveh conquered the world of its day. Concerning this city and nation God makes some very specific declarations. He says, "But with an overrunning flood he will make an utter end of the place thereof . . . . I will make thy grave; for thou art vile." The prophet said as he looked into the future, "She is empty, and void, and waste: . . . no more of thy name be sown." Interesting prophecies. What happened? Nineveh was taken away, just as God had said.

Nahum 1:8, 14

Nahum 2:10

Nahum 1:14

How was this done? Exactly in the manner that God had prophesied. Nahum the prophet declared, ". . . they shall make haste to the wall thereof, and the defence shall be prepared. The gates of the rivers shall be opened, and the palace shall be dissolved." Further, ". . . the gates of thy land shall be set wide open unto thy enemies: the fire shall devour thy bars." Notice the details of these prophecies. The Ninevites are to flee in haste to the great defensive walls of their city which are prepared for any attack. But the gates of the rivers shall be opened and shall dissolve the palace. This results in the gates of the land being set wide

Nahum 2:5, 6

Nahum 3:13

open to the enemies and fire devouring the city. The only detailed historical account of the fall of Nineveh is the account of Ctesias, preserved in *Diodorus Siculus*. According to that account, Cyaxares (the Median monarch) aided by the Babylonians under Nabopolassar, laid siege to the city. His first efforts were in vain. He was more than once repulsed and was obliged to take refuge in the mountains of the Zagros Range; but, receiving reinforcements, he succeeded in routing the Assyrian army and driving them to shut themselves up within the walls. He then attempted to reduce the city by blockade, but was unsuccessful for two years till his efforts were unexpectedly assisted by an extraordinary rise of the Tigris which swept away a part of the walls and rendered it possible for the Medes to enter. The Assyrian monarch, Saracus, in despair burned himself in his palace. With the ruthless barbarity of the times, the conquerors gave the whole city over to the flames and razed its former magnificence to the ground (*Cyclopedia of Biblical Theological and Ecclesiastical Literature,* vol. 7, p. 112). God makes clear that the destruction of this city will be total and irremediable. He says, "But with an overrunning flood he will make an *utter end* to the place thereof, and darkness shall pursue his enemies." The city was then laid waste, its monuments destroyed, and its inhabitants scattered or carried away into captivity. It never rose again from its ruins. This total disappearance of Nineveh is fully confirmed by the records of history.

Nahum 1:8

The prophet Nahum also said of Nineveh, "She is empty, and void, and waste . . . ." The skeptic Edward Gibbon described the complete fulfillment of this prophecy when he detailed a battle fought on the very site where once Nineveh had stood. He said that eastward of the Tigris, at the end of the bridge of Mosul, the great Nineveh had formerly been erected: the city, and even the ruins, had long since disappeared; the vacant space afforded spacious field for the operation of the two armies (*Gibbon's History,* vol. 8, pp. 250, 251). God had also said, "I will make thy grave; for thou art vile." The mounds show neither bricks, stones, nor other materials of building: but are in many places overgrown with grass (*Buckingham's Travels in Mesopotamia,* vol. 2, p. 49). God had said that He would literally wipe Nineveh off the face of the earth and make an utter end of it. In unknowing confirmation of the fulfillment of that prophecy, Constantin Volney cries, "Where

Nahum 2:10

Nahum 1:14

Nahum 1:9

are those ramparts of Nineveh? The name of Nineveh
seems to be threatened with the same oblivion that has
overtaken its greatness" (*Volney's Ruins,* chaps. 2, 4). E. A.
Rowell has said that never had the world seen such a city.
Its great rampart walls towered upward two hundred feet
and on top several chariots could race abreast. Gleaming in
the sun, its lofty palaces and temple towers stabbed the sky
above the towering walls and thrilled the approaching
traveler while he was yet miles away.

The city was so completely destroyed, that the Romans in
A.D. 627 under Heraclius fought a battle on top of Nineveh
and didn't even know it was there, and for well over a
thousand years few people even believed that it had ever
existed. As recently as 1840, the writings of skeptics are
filled with delusions that Nineveh and·Sargon and Ashur-
banipal, the great kings of Assyria, are all mythological
characters—some of the many mistakes of the Bible
—because, as every educated person knows, Nineveh

Nahum 3:17
Nahum 1:14

never existed, Assyria never was. ". . . their place is not
known . . . that no more of thy name be sown." It wasn't
until 1840 that someone discovered a brick in the midst of
the mounds near the Tigris River that had on it the name of
Sargon, King of Assyria. This was taken to the Paris
Museum where they said it was obviously a fraud because
everybody knows there was no Nineveh, so there was no
Sargon! But in 1845 Layard, who was to become the greatest
Assyriologist of all time, had the audacity to uncover the
palace, the library, and the whole city. The critics were
forced to admit that Nineveh had existed after all.

Consider the magnificent kingdom that followed it:
Babylonia. Babylon was probably the greatest city that was
ever built. Here was the magnificent temple of Belus; and
here were the world famous Hanging Gardens.

She drew her stores from no foreign country. She invented an alphabet; worked out problems of arithmetic;
invented implements for measuring time; conceived the
plan of building enormous structures with the poorest of all
materials—clay; discovered the art of polishing, boring,
and engraving gems; studied successfully the motions of
the heavenly bodies; conceived of grammar as a science;
elaborated a system of law; saw the value of exact chronol-
ogy. In almost every branch of science, she made a beginning. Much of the art and learning of Greece came from
Babylon. But of this majestic kingdom, this Babylon the

Golden, God said, ". . . Babylon, the glory of kingdoms, the beauty of the Chaldees excellency, shall be as when God overthrew Sodom and Gomorrah." This is but one of over one hundred specific prophecies that are made concerning Babylon alone. The specificity of these prophecies is so great that they cannot possibly be said to be obscure as in the Delphic Oracles. Nor can they be said to have been written after the event, because many of the details of the prophecy were not fulfilled until centuries after the Septuagint translation of the Hebrew Old Testament into Greek in 150 B.C. It is not possible to give a later date for these prophecies. Nor can it be said that they have not been fulfilled for any school boy with a good encyclopedia can ascertain that they have been minutely fulfilled. In these prophecies concerning the future of great cities and kingdoms, God has written His imprimatur in the Scriptures, confirming them as divine revelations in such bold letters that He that runneth may read. Nor can it be said that they are simply lucky guesses, because there are thousands of such prophecies in the Scriptures which have been minutely fulfilled. Nor yet can it be said that they concern events which were likely to take place. Indeed, many of the events were totally without precedence in the history of the world and were so incredible and unbelievable in their very nature, that even though history has fully confirmed them to be true, we still stagger at the audacity of the prophets who made such bold statements.

Consider the great walls of Babylon. Herodotus tells us that these walls had towers which extended above the two-hundred-foot walls to a height of three hundred feet. The walls were a hundred-eighty-seven feet thick at the base and were fourteen miles square, according to one ancient authority. The triple walls of Babylon were the mightiest walls that were ever built around any city. Concerning these walls God says, in Jeremiah 51:58, "The broad walls of Babylon shall be utterly broken . . . ." Also, "And they shall not take of thee a stone for a corner, nor a stone for foundations; but thou shalt be desolate for ever." Consider these astounding facts. (1) The wall is to be broken down, (2) it is to be broken down completely, (3) it is to be broken down permanently. It cannot possibly be said that these prophecies did not come to pass. Even the skeptics attest their fulfillment. "Where are the walls of Babylon?" asks Constantin Volney in his *Ruins*. Major

Isaiah 13:19

Psalms 147:15

Jeremiah 51:58

Jeremiah 51:26

Keppel said in his *Narrative* that in common with other travelers, we totally failed in discovering any trace of the city walls.

Nor can anyone say that the prophecy was made after the event, for the walls were not suddenly destroyed. The city was taken by stealth by the Medes and Persians and the destruction of her walls was a slow process that took centuries. The walls were still in existence in the time of Alexander the Great. They still jutted into the sky at the time of Christ. In the fourth century A.D., some remains of the walls were still there, a stark reminder that the prophecy had not yet been completely fulfilled. Then the most astounding event took place. Julian the Apostate, Emperor of Rome, determined to rid the Roman Empire of Christianity and reestablish paganism was doing all in his power to destroy belief in the Scriptures. However, God had said

Psalms 76:10

that even "the wrath of man shall praise [Him]." While engaged in a war with the Persians near the remains of Babylon (although he had no idea of the prophecy that he was fulfilling), Julian completely destroyed the remnants of the wall of Babylon lest it afford any protection in the future for the Persian army. And thus the prophecy was brought to fulfillment by one of the greatest antagonists of Scripture of all time.

One cannot say it was inevitable that the wall would be destroyed. The Great Wall of China is not nearly as large or as strong, and yet, though it is older, it still stands today. The walls of Jerusalem and many other ancient cities, though destroyed many times in part, have been rebuilt

Jeremiah 39:8
Daniel 9:25
Micah 7:11
Isaiah 33:20

and still remain to our time. I have personally walked atop the great walls of Jerusalem, which God said would be destroyed, but also He said that they would be built again in troublous times. In the case of the Babylonian wall and the Jerusalem wall, exactly what God said has come to pass.

When Babylon was the mistress of the world, containing within its mighty walls one hundred ninety-six square miles of the most magnificently developed city of all time, with beautiful parks, lakes, aqueducts, and hanging gardens, the prophet Jeremiah made this astounding

Jeremiah 50:13

prophecy: "Because of the wrath of the Lord it shall not be inhabited, but it shall be wholly desolate." Even more astonishing is the further prophecy of Jeremiah: ". . . and it shall be no more inhabited for ever; neither shall it be

Jeremiah 50:39

dwelt in from generation to generation." This was an astonishing prophecy, for it was virtually without precedent. Many ancient cities in the Near East had been destroyed, but always they had been built again on the ruins of the previous cities. There is evidence of sometimes twenty or thirty cities being built on the very same site. Babylon was most excellently situated on the Euphrates. It had fine possibilities of commerce. It was militarily almost invincible. Its fields were so fertile that Herodotus, having visited there, was afraid to describe what he saw lest he be thought insane.

Have these astonishing prophecies been fulfilled? Babylon was described as the tenantless and desolate metropolis (*Mignan's Travels,* p. 234), a barren desert in which the ruins were nearly the only indication that it had been inhabited. Regarding Babylon, Isaiah said, "Nor dwelt in from generation to generation." In the sixteenth century, there was not a house to be seen at Babylon (*Ray's Collection of Travels,* Rawolf, p. 174). In the nineteenth century, it is still desolate and tenantless (Mignan, p. 284). In the twentieth century, ruins are all that remain of the once magnificent city where King Belshazzar saw the handwriting on the wall (John Elder, *Prophets and Diggers,* p. 106). "It shall never be inhabited," prophesied Isaiah. Ruins composed like those of Babylon of heaps of rubbish impregnated with niter cannot be cultivated (*Rich's Memoirs,* p. 16). The decomposing materials of a Babylonian structure doom the earth on which they perish to a lasting sterility (*Sir R. K. Porter's Travels,* vol. 2, p. 391). Thus God guaranteed the fulfillment of His prophecies. ". . . thou [Babylon] shalt be desolate for ever. Babylon shall become heaps, a dwelling place for dragons, an astonishment, and an hissing, without an inhabitant."

There are other amazingly specific details in this prophecy. Consider this detail: ". . . neither shall the Arabian pitch tent there." Has this come true? Captain Mignan said that he saw the sun sink behind the Mujelibah, and obeyed with infinite regret the summons of his guides who were completely armed. He could not persuade them to remain longer. From the apprehension of evil spirits it is impossible to eradicate this idea from the minds of these people (*Mignan's Travels,* pp. 2, 198, 201). Continues Isaiah: "Neither shall the shepherds make their fold there." All the people of the country assert that it is extremely dangerous to approach this mound after night fall

Isaiah 13:20

Isaiah 13:20

Jeremiah 51:26, 37

Isaiah 13:20

on account of the multitude of evil spirits by which it is haunted. By this superstitious belief they are prevented from pitching a tent by night or making a fold (*Rich's Memoirs*, p. 27).

Consider these two specific but apparently contradictory prophecies. "The sea is come up upon Babylon: she is covered with the multitude of the waves thereof." And, ". . . a desolation, a dry land and a wilderness." Now note the amazing fulfillment: For the space of two months throughout the year the ruins of Babylon are inundated by the annual overflowing of the Euphrates so as to render many parts of them inaccessible by converting the valleys into morasses (*Rich's Memoirs*, p. 13). After the subsiding of the waters, even the low heaps become again sunburnt ruins and the sight of Babylon like that of the other cities of Chaldea is a dry waste, a parched and burning plain (*Buckingham's Travels*, vol. 2, pp. 302–305).

In spite of the unimaginable fertility of the plains around Babylon, God had said, "Cut off the sower from Babylon, and him that handleth the sickle in the time of harvest . . . ." On this part of the plain both where traces of buildings were left and where none had stood, all seemed equally naked of vegetation (*Porter's Travels*, vol. 2, p. 392). "And Babylon shall become heaps." And again, ". . . cast her up as heaps, and destroy her utterly: let nothing of her be left." Babylon has become a vast succession of mounds; a great mass of ruined heaps. Vast heaps constitute all that now remains of ancient Babylon (*Keppel's Narrative*, vol. 1, p. 196).

These prophecies are presented here as examples of the over one hundred specific prophecies relating to the city of Babylon. The wrath of the Lord was poured out upon Babylon. God said, "The Lord . . . will do his pleasure on Babylon. . . . for every purpose of the Lord shall be performed against Babylon. And I will bring upon that land all my words which I have pronounced against it, even all that is written in this book . . . ." Let us close this discussion of Babylon with the words of one who looked with his own eyes upon the fulfillment of these prophecies. "I cannot portray," says Captain Mignan, "the overpowering sensation of reverential awe that possessed my mind while contemplating the extent and magnitude of ruin and devastation on every side" (*Mignan's Travels*, p. 117).

Jeremiah 51:42
Jeremiah 51:43
Jeremiah 50:16
Jeremiah 51:37
Jeremiah 50:26
Isaiah 48:14
Jeremiah 51:29
Jeremiah 25:13

Thus God threw down the gauntlet to all unbelievers. Do you want to disprove the Scriptures? It is very easy! Simply rebuild Babylon! God said it shall never be inhabited; it shall never be rebuilt, but it would always remain a desolation. There was a man who set out to rebuild it. I should tell you about him. He had all of the wealth of the whole world at his command. His name was Alexander the Great. After conquering the world, he decided to have a trade route by sea from Babylon to Egypt, and he decided to make Babylon his central headquarters for his worldwide empire. He issued six hundred thousand rations to his soldiers to rebuild the city of Babylon. Alexander the Great, the ruler of the world, said, "Rebuild Babylon!" and God struck him dead! He was immediately taken with a fever and within a few days he was dead. The ruins of Babylon still stand in mute testimony. "I, the Lord, have spoken it! It shall never be inhabited again!"

Jeremiah 50:39

Compare these prophecies of destruction with what the Bible says about Egypt. God said that Nineveh, Assyria, and Babylonia would be completely destroyed and not be rebuilt. What if He had said that about Egypt? Ah, how the skeptics would laugh. But He didn't. ". . . they shall be there a base kingdom. It shall be the basest of the kingdoms; neither shall it exalt itself any more above the nations: for I will diminish them, that they shall no more rule over the nations. . . . the pride of her power shall come down . . . . And they shall be desolate in the midst of the countries that are desolate, and her cities shall be in the midst of the cities that are wasted. And I will make the land of Egypt desolate. . . . and the country shall be destitute of that whereof it was full. And I will . . . sell the land into the hand of the wicked: and I will make the land waste, and all that is therein, by the hand of strangers: I the Lord have spoken it. . . . and there shall be no more a prince of the land of Egypt."

Ezekiel 29:14, 15

Ezekiel 30:6, 7

Ezekiel 29:12
Ezekiel 32:15

Ezekiel 30:13

Ezekiel 24:14
Ezekiel 30:13

Let us note that the fate of Egypt is not, as in the case of Nineveh and Babylon, to be utter extinction, but rather "they shall be there." Egypt was to continue to exist as a nation but "a base nation." "The basest of nations." It is to be diminished and emptied of that whereof it was full. Have these prophecies been fulfilled? After the defeat of Antony, Augustus found such great wealth in Egypt that he paid out of it all of the arrears of his army and all of the

Ezekiel 29:14, 15

debts that he had incurred during the war. Still he feared that the wealth of Egypt would present to him a rival. For six hundred more years Alexandria continued to be the first city in the Roman Empire in rank, commerce, and prosperity. A hundred years later the Muslim hordes attacked Egypt and conquered it. They were overwhelmed by the sight of the city's magnificence and wealth. Future invaders were equally astonished at the wealth of Egypt, until the nation was reduced to a state of abject poverty, finally being brought to the place of international bankruptcy which brought about the Anglo-French dominion of Egypt.

Ezekiel 30:13

One of the most astonishing parts of the prophecy is the statement, "There shall be no more a prince of the land of Egypt." This prophecy is particularly striking when we note that for approximately two thousand years before the prophecy was made, Egypt had had Egyptian princes sitting upon its throne. It seemed as if it would continue forever. But God declares that there shall no more be a prince of the land of Egypt. What a startling declaration! There has been ample time for the testing of the prophecy, for there continued to be a prince on the throne of Egypt until the last several decades when a democratic form of government was accepted. But were any of these princes Egyptians? Let us have that question answered by the pens of skeptics and infidels. Constantin Volney said that deprived two thousand three hundred years ago of her natural proprietors, Egypt has seen her fertile fields successively a prey to the Persians, the Macedonians, the Romans, the Greeks, the Arabs, the Georgians, and at length the race of Tartars, distinguished by the name of Ottoman Turks, the Mamelukes soon usurped the power and elected a leader (*Volney's Travels*, vol. 1, pp. 74, 103, 110, 193). After Volney's time, Mohammed Ali established the princedom again in Egypt but he, himself, was not an Egyptian. Rather he was born at Kavala, a small seaport on the frontier of Thrace and Macedonia. His father was an Albanian aga. After this, Egypt was ruled by the French and the English. The skeptic Edward Gibbon confirms this testimony where he states that a more unjust and absurd constitution cannot be devised than that which condemns the natives of a country to perpetual servitude under the arbitrary dominion of strangers and slaves (Gibbon, *The Decline and Fall of the Roman Empire*, chap. 59).

Today, Egypt, which has for two millennia suffered under the despotic hand of strangers, has been reduced to one of the basest of nations. My guide to the Holy Land a few years ago said that he had been to Egypt thirty or forty times, but he was never going back again because it was so foul, so vile smelling, so poverty ridden that he couldn't stand another trip. His stomach couldn't take the cities of Egypt any more. "I will make thee the basest of nations."

Ezekiel 29:14, 15

These are but a few of the thousands of prophecies with which the Scripture abounds, which are found in no other religious writings of the world, and which are clear evidence that the Scripture has been written by the hand of God.

> How firm a foundation, ye saints of the Lord,
> Is laid for your faith in his excellent Word!
> What more can he say than to you He hath said?

Isaiah 46:9

"I am He that declareth the end from the beginning and from former times things which have not yet come to pass. . . . I am God and there is none like me, Declaring the end from the beginning, and from ancient times the things that are not yet done." "Hereby ye will know the prophet is come from Me because he will tell the future," as the Bible and no other book, unfailingly and infallibly, does. The Scriptures are the Word of God. "Sanctify them through thy truth," said Christ, "thy word is truth."

Isaiah 46:9, 10

Deuteronomy 18:22

John 17:17

"The Scriptures cannot be broken!"

SCRIPTURE INDEX

SCRIPTURE INDEX

157